Deck & Patio Upgrades

Created by the Editorial Staff of Ortho Books

**Project Director
& Writer**

Karin Shakery

Illustrator

Richard Moore

Ortho Books

Publisher
Edward A. Evans

Editorial Director
Christine Jordan

Production Director
Ernie S. Tasaki

Managing Editors
Robert J. Beckstrom
Michael D. Smith
Sally W. Smith

System Manager
Linda M. Bouchard

Product Manager
Richard E. Pile, Jr.

Distribution Specialist
Barbara F. Steadham

Operations Assistant
Georgiann Wright

Administrative Assistant
Francine Lorentz-Olson

Technical Consultant
J. A. Crozier, Jr., Ph.D.

Address all inquiries to:
Ortho Books
Chevron Chemical Company
Consumer Products Division
Box 5047
San Ramon, CA 94583

ISBN 0-89721-225-8
Library of Congress Catalog Card Number 90-80070

Chevron Chemical Company
6001 Bollinger Canyon Road, San Ramon, CA 94583

Acknowledgments

Designers
Mark Becker, Becker & Associates, Mill Valley, CA: Page 38 (below)
Anthony Bertotti Landscaping, Novato, CA: Pages 6–7
Warren & Chula Camp, San Francisco, CA: Pages 18–19
Milt Charno & Associates, Hales Corners, WI: Page 57
Helen Craddick, Cole-Wheatman Designers, San Francisco, CA: Page 21
Robert Engman, Mill Valley, CA: Page 23
Lorenzo Foncerrada, San Diego, CA: Page 22
John Hemingway, Los Altos, CA: Page 56
Christian Kilka, Kiillkkaa Group Landscape Artisans, San Francisco, CA: Page 103
Don Knorr & Associates, San Francisco, CA: Page 39 (below)
John Matthias, San Anselmo, CA: Pages 8, 89
David Nelson and Jan Bauman, Mill Valley, CA: Page 16 (above)
William Picardi, Picardi Construction, Southborough, MA: Page 10
Milton L. Sandy, Jr. Corinth, MI: Pages 34–35
Santa Barbara Water Gardens & Landscapes, Santa Barbara, CA: Page 14 Sasaki Associates, San Francisco, Los Angeles, and Santa Ana, CA: Pages 15 and 16 (left)
Mark Scott, Newport Beach, CA: Page 37 (above)
Karin Shakery, Mill Valley, CA: Page 76–77, 78–79, 101, 104–105, 108–109
L. Dennis Shields, Dana Point, CA: Pages 54–5
Eli Sutton, Rohnert Park, CA: Cover, Pages 38 (above), 39 (above)
Timberline Design Group, San Diego, CA: Page 59

Sources
California Redwood Association
Western Wood Products Association
American Plywood Association
Diane Snow
William H. W. Wilson

Photographers
Mark Becker: Pages 10, 38 (below)
Laurie Black: Pages 18–19, 20, 21, 58, 61
Ernest Braun: Pages 8, 38 (above), 39, 89
Kim Brun: Pages 54–55
Saxon Holt: Pages 1, 3, 12, 14, 16, 37 (below), 90, 94
Michael Landis: Page 13
George Lyons: Pages 22, 57, 59
Ortho Library: Pages 88 (top), 91
Tom Rider: Cover, page 56
Karl Riek: Page 23
Renee Carver Robinson Photography: Pages 6–7, 15, 16 (left), 37 (above)
Karin Shakery: Pages 16, 86–87, 88 (below)

Additional Illustrators
Ron Hildebrand: Pages 17, 42
Rik Olson: Pages 21, 33, 41
Kathryn Williamson: Pages 24–28

Composition by
Laurie Steele

Production by
Billie Webb
Lezlly Freier

Separations by
Color Tech. Corp.

Lithographed in the USA by
Webcrafters, Inc.

Front Cover: Plenty of seating is a must for any deck or patio. To avoid cluttering up the space with lots of furniture, the owners of this hillside lot clad a retaining wall with redwood and used it as a backrest for a bench that extends the full width. For more information on building the wall, see page 31. To get ideas for building benches, see pages 70 to 73.

Page 1: The juxtaposition of hard and soft textures makes this brick patio a pleasant spot for relaxing in the sunshine. Brick laid in a basket weave pattern flows into a lush carpet of grass and wistfia climbs up support posts of the shingle-roofed passageway. To lay brick in a basket weave pattern work in rows. Work down the first row, placing two horizontal bricks next to two vertical ones. On the second row, reverse the order—place two vertical bricks next to two horizontal ones. Complete the patio alternating these two rows. For more on laying brick, see pages 12 to 13.

Page 3: The walls that mark the boundaries of your outdoor living space should provide privacy without making you feel imprisoned. In this house, guests get a sense of what is beyond the gate but not a full view. End posts of the fence double as a frame for the gate and a support for the roof structure. For more on setting posts, see pages 24 to 29.

Back cover: This book contains illustrations and instructions for making numerous projects. The four shown are the gazebo (see pages 48 to 53), a swing made with pieces of dowel (see pages 74 to 75), a redwood planter (see page 102), and an entrance lanai (see page 47).

Deck & Patio Upgrades

FURNISHING OUTDOOR SPACE

This book assumes that you already have a structurally sound deck or a patio in good repair. In other words, you have a well-planned open area, but one that needs to be turned into comfortable outdoor living space. If this is not the case, pick up a copy of Ortho's "How to Design & Build Decks & Patios" or "Deck Plans."

What you will find in this book is a wealth of ideas on how to spruce up and furnish your deck or patio. There are numerous photographs to inspire you and illustrations accompanied by step-by-step directions on how to build a variety of projects. (Some of these are seen on these pages.)

When preparing this book, we talked to many people about design trends and changing attitudes about outdoor living. The California Redwood Association notes a trend away from ordinary, square, or rectangular decks. "Modern decks are often asymmetrical, with shapes that complement the house design," they say. "Also seen are changing levels with artful transitions from one platform to another. Deck railings are becoming more sophisticated, often designed with ornate shapes, latticework, or painted elements. Modern decks are loaded with amenities—privacy screens, food preparation and serving centers, built-in benches, gazebos, spas, planters, shade trellises, and exterior lighting—that truly personalize them and make them enjoyable for many activities."

The Western Wood Association has also noticed an increased awareness in how people use outdoor areas: "With the growing popularity of decks—something like a million and a half of them being built every year—two trends seem to be emerging. In the new home market, decks are almost routinely designed and built as part of a home instead of merely being tacked on afterward. Consequently, they reflect and complement the style of the house. Second, in the existing home market, many of the decks being added are far more elaborate. They are larger, frequently on multiple levels, and feature amenities such as gazebos, arbors, spas, built-in barbecues, and potting benches. Our field representatives have noticed a rapidly growing interest in what we call the three-season porch. This is a deck with walls and a roof added to part or all of it. These porches retain the feeling of a full view and openness but add some protection from the elements. No attempt is made to disguise the fact that they are still essentially decks. They are simply somewhat more elaborate versions that can be used for a longer season."

These statements confirm our belief that people are treating outdoor areas as living rooms. Because of this, the chapter titles reflect the steps taken when designing interior space. We talk about floors, walls, roofs, furniture, and color schemes. Translated into outdoor vernacular the chapter titles refer to decking and paving, fences and walls, overhead structures, outdoor furnishings, and planters.

Many of the projects in this book require a knowledge of building techniques in addition to carpentry skills. Therefore, you will find guidelines on how to install outdoor wiring, how to set a post, how to attach a ledger, and how to install an irrigation system. These sections are included so that the lamppost on page 64 will light, so that you can attach the overhead structure on page 44, and so that flowers will bloom profusely in the planters that start on page 96.

FLOORS: A STAGE FOR OUTDOOR LIVING

The surface of your existing deck or patio may be in disrepair or may not suit the additions you expect to make, or you just may not like it. Whatever the case, this chapter contains ideas for installing new flooring.

The ability to refigure a deck depends on the support structure, and generally this will limit your choices to merely changing the appearance of the decking boards. This might involve replacing them or painting, staining, or bleaching them.

On an existing patio, your choices are a lot broader. Maybe you have an ordinary-looking slab that would look much better covered with brick, flagstone, pavers, or a new, more decorative concrete surface. Or you might consider breaking up the slab to simulate the look of flagstones.

When resurfacing a patio, you are not limited by a support structure, but you will have to make changes around the perimeter. The new covering must be contained by an edging.

A circular patio is linked to other areas with paths that swirl around the side of the house. When laying brick in a circle pattern, butt bottom corners of bricks and allow a slight gap at top corners. This gap will become more exaggerated as you near the center and the diameter of the circle becomes smaller. When the gaps become too large, knock the corners off bricks.

IDEAS FOR RENEWING DECKS

The structure supporting your deck is going to determine what changes you can make. But there is no limit to how creative you can get with paint, stain, and bleach.

Deck Boards

Before deciding on decking changes, it is extremely important to make sure that the basic structure is in good repair. And while you are checking, make sure that the structure is also strong enough to support whatever you plan to put on top of the decking. If there will be a large planter on the deck, the area underneath should be reinforced with extra sleepers and, if necessary, extra posts.

Obviously, it is impossible to lay boards in an entirely different direction unless you are willing to make extensive joist changes or additions. But you could place one of the modules shown on page 11 in such a way that boards run perpendicular or at a diagonal to existing ones.

Opposite: Building around a tree necessitates careful planning and a lot of measuring and cutting. But the end result is a naturally shaded deck area with a lot of interest. These redwood steps are wide enough and deep enough to double as benches. Note how the miter-cut facing on each step matches the planking on the planter. This sort of attention to detail is what distinguishes a well executed project.

Transitions

Adding steps or platforms to an existing deck can completely change its aspect. As well as making a visual difference, these transitions will expand the way you use your deck.

Plan steps that improve traffic flow. For example, providing better access to the kitchen simplifies serving food outdoors. And linking the deck with the yard allows children to play while adults relax. If you have enough space, linking two levels with platforms is much better than building steps. Platforms descend more gradually, creating a softer contour. They can also serve as separate seating, dining, or play areas.

Preserving Wood

The Environmental Protection Agency has banned a number of preservatives from over-the-counter sales and restricted their use to licensed applicators and manufacturers of pressure-treated lumber. The restricted list currently includes creosote, pentachlorophenols, and inorganic arsenic compounds. Other preservatives may soon be added to this list.

Since the restricted preservatives are not available to homeowners, you do not have to worry about handling them.

However, there are risks involved with lumber that is already treated. Use lumber treated with pentachlorophenol for structural members only or treat the lumber with two coats of a nonpreservative sealer. Avoid creosote-treated lumber altogether. Lumber treated with inorganic arsenic compounds (chromated copper arsenate, for example) can be used on deck boards and railings. Do not place food on preservative-treated lumber or use it on a surface where your skin will come in contact with the wood for a prolonged period. All restrictions and recommendations may change; therefore, check with a reliable retailer or a local environmental authority before buying a preservative.

When you work with pressure-treated lumber, take safety precautions. Wear goggles and a respirator. Wear gloves if the wood is damp. When you finish the job, do not burn leftover scraps of wood. Dispose of them in a dumping site that handles hazardous waste.

Restoring Wood

A deck composed of darkened, stained boards will look entirely different (and larger) if you clean the wood using any of the numerous products available at home center stores. Apply, following the manufacturer's directions and precautions. Sometimes, just scrubbing the boards with water is

as effective as these products. Test a small area before spending your money on cleansers.

You can also use oxalic acid to brighten or restore the natural color of wood. If you do so, be sure to wear gloves, protective clothing, and safety goggles. Also protect surrounding areas, plants, and shrubbery.

Coloring Decks

If both the structure and the decking are in good condition, the simplest way to achieve a new look is with color. Paint, stain, or bleach will give your deck a brand-new look.

Painting Boards

Painting is an easy way to give a deck a brand-new lease on life, and new formulas have greatly increased the number of products for painting exterior floors. Choices are no longer limited to red and green. Check out the products available at local paint stores and ask for advice on the necessary preparation steps for your particular surface.

The deck can be painted a solid color, or you might try painting just a few boards to create a border around a particular area.

Staining Boards

If you prefer to add color rather than bleach it out, you can find a wide variety of stains in traditional wood colors as well as a range of both translucent- and opaque-colored stains.

Interesting angles and steps direct the visitor down to a large expanse of lawn. Planters, acting as barriers, mark the position of the steps.

Bleaching Boards

Bleach is a popular finish for indoor wood, and there is no reason why you can't also bleach deck boards.

You can bleach wood with chlorinated household bleach, bleaching oil, or commercial wood bleach.

Household bleach is the mildest and safest to use. Dilute one part bleach with one part water. If used full strength, bleach may produce a yellowish or greenish tinge (which you might find attractive). Household bleach can be neutralized with white vinegar used full strength or with soap and water.

If household bleach doesn't give you the desired effect, you can use bleach oil. Apply according to manufacturer's recommendations. Directions often specify that the product needs six months of weathering before its full effect is realized.

Commercial wood bleach is the strongest bleach available for wood, and it is applied in two separate solutions: The first usually consists of sodium silicate or lye, the second of concentrated hydrogen peroxide. Use both solutions with great care and follow the manufacturer's directions exactly.

DUCKBOARDS

The original duckboard was used as a raised platform or floor over a wet or muddy area. You can also use these modules to sculpture a flat deck or patio.

Making Duckboards

Different heights and levels are much more interesting than a flat plane, and a change of level is easy to accomplish by adding duckboards. They can be used as steps, for seating, as tables, or to raise planters to a more pleasing height. Easy to carry and reposition, they can be made in the workshop and then moved to the site.

If you plan to cover an entire patio area, nail scraps of ½-inch plywood to both sides of each corner. (See illustration.) These will provide air circulation gaps if modules are grouped together. If you are building several modules, it is worth making a nailing jig. (See illustration.)

This duckboard is 35½ inches square and made from 2 by 4s, but you can build it to a different size or shape. If you want a larger version, just add more support cleats. If you prefer to reduce the weight, use 1 by 4 lumber for the decking and center a third cleat between the outer two. If you like the look of narrower boards, use 2 by 3s or 2 by 2s.

For maximum strength and longevity, use structural grade, pressure-treated lumber for the cleats. (Wear safety goggles, gloves, and a breathing mask whenever you cut pressure-treated lumber.)

Materials Required

Construction grade, pressure-treated 2×4 cleats
Lengths of 2×4 decking boards
10d box nails
Scrap lumber for nailing jig (optional)
Scrap ½" plywood (optional)

Constructing a Duckboard

Cut 9 decking boards and 2 cleats 35½ inches long.

If you will be using a jig, make it out of pieces of lumber nailed into a 35½-inch square (inside measurements).

Lay out decking boards, allowing ½ inch space between. Lay cleats across top and bottom of boards and hammer 2 nails through cleat into each end of board. To avoid splitting wood, drill pilot holes or blunt ends of nails before nailing.

If modules will be grouped, nail plywood scraps to corners.

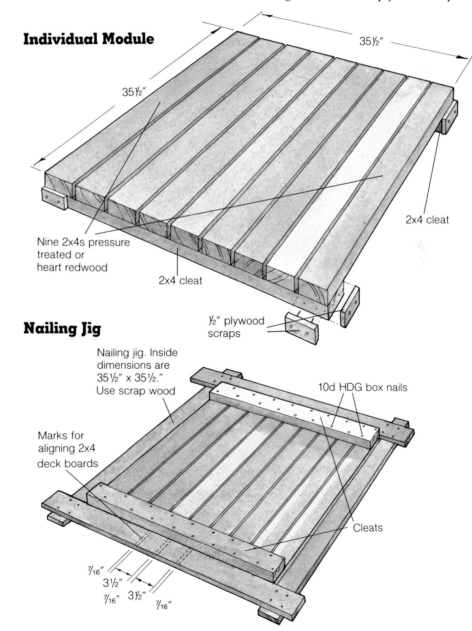

Individual Module

35½"

35½"

2x4 cleat

Nine 2x4s pressure treated or heart redwood

2x4 cleat

½" plywood scraps

Nailing Jig

Nailing jig. Inside dimensions are 35½" x 35½." Use scrap wood

10d HDG box nails

Marks for aligning 2x4 deck boards

Cleats

⁷⁄₁₆"   3½"   ⁷⁄₁₆"   3½"   ⁷⁄₁₆"

IDEAS FOR RENEWING PATIO SURFACES

Changing the look of a patio offers many more flooring options than renewing a deck. Because you are at ground level, additional support is not a problem. However, it is important to start with a clean, level base.

Brick

Brick is one of the easiest paving materials to work with and provides quick and satisfying results. It is not even necessary to lay bricks in mortar as long as you have a well-compacted and reasonably level surface.

If you are laying bricks on an existing slab, the following brick-on-sand method is perfectly satisfactory even in areas of the country that experience severe frost. (If you live in such an area, bricks will heave if the sand base is poured on top of earth.)

Laying Bricks in Sand

Build an edging around area to contain brick; then, within this area, spread a bed of sand approximately 2 inches deep.

Press bricks into sand and tamp to level them. Use a large piece of plywood when kneeling on bricks that have already been positioned.

When entire area is bricked, spread more sand on top and sweep it into cracks. Water entire surface to settle it and sweep in more sand. Repeat watering and sweeping until all cracks are completely filled.

Laying Bricks in Mortar

If you prefer to lay bricks in mortar for either practical or aesthetic reasons, refer to the section Laying Flagstone on page 15 for basic guidelines.

A herringbone pattern is one of the most popular for laying brick. It does involve a lot of cutting at ends of lines. However, if you have a situation like this patio, uneven ends can be disguised by using stones to form the edge of the planting bed.

Bricks do not have to be set in mortar in order to provide an attractive floor. This idyllic lakefront patio was set on a sand base. However, it is necessary to cement a border around the perimeter of the patio to hold the sand in place. Bricks around the cutout for the tree are also set in cement. When building around a tree, give it some breathing room. If you extend paving too close to the trunk, the tree will not get enough water and roots will break the paving.

Flagstone

If you have an existing patio surface that does not please you, consider paving it with flagstone. Laying flagstone is a time-consuming and back-breaking project but not a difficult one.

Spacing the stones depends on the effect you wish to achieve, that is, the proportion of stone to mortar. It also depends on how much time you are prepared to put into finding stones that fit well together. (If you enjoy doing jigsaw puzzles, you will enjoy laying stone.) Once you are satisfied with the layout, you are ready to set stones in mortar. Because you will need a stiff mortar mix, you must work quickly in fairly small sections before it dries out.

Laying Flagstone

First do a careful layout finding stones that fit together well.

Remove 2 or 3 stones and spread a bed of mortar about 1 inch thick. (Use more if stones are very irregular.) Mix mortar using 1 part portland cement to 3 parts masonry sand. Keep mix fairly stiff so it will support stones. Position a stone and tamp to seat it.

Continue spreading mortar and laying stones using a large piece of plywood when kneeling on stones that have already been set. Allow mortar to cure for at least 24 hours.

Trowel on mortar to fill joints. Work carefully, spilling as little as possible. If you do get mortar on the surface of the stone, wipe it up immediately with a sponge dipped frequently in clean water.

Concrete

Concrete is one of the most versatile building materials. Unfortunately it has a reputation for being strictly utilitarian. This need not be the case. With creativity in an appropriate location, patios surfaced with textured concrete, exposed aggregate, concrete pavers, and even broken concrete can be extremely good looking as well as eminently practical.

Resurfacing a Slab

Before you pour (place) new concrete directly on top of an existing slab, the surface must be cleaned and scarified (roughed up). This procedure calls for renting a machine that chips off the top surface.

Rather than going to this trouble, a much easier way to add a new layer of concrete is to lay 6 mil polyethylene on top of the existing surface, add a layer of sand if you need to smooth out the level, and pour the new concrete on top.

Realize that by pouring a new slab you will be increasing the height of your patio by approximately three inches (the depth of the pour). Be sure to install new edging and allow for expansion joints.

After the concrete is poured, the finish floating is done with different tools, depending on the final texture you want. The final finish must be done while the concrete is still wet but after it has set up slightly—when the sheen of water on the surface has disappeared. In hot, dry weather this may take only a few minutes.

Above: A sloped bank is turned into a series of planted terraces that spill down to the patio paved with concrete aggregate. See page 16 for information on this and other concrete finishes. For more about retaining walls, see page 30. Opposite: Reminiscent of a farmhouse in Provence, this stone patio is instantly refreshing. The pool is ringed by a stone patio with a free-form edge. Large pieces of stone are set in mortar, with rocks embedded around them. The same stone is used on the steps that lead to the sitting room, and rocks are pressed into the risers.

Above: Concrete pavers do not necessarily create a hard landscape. Here, they are set far enough apart for a ground cover to grow between them, creating the look of stepping-stones rather than of an area covered with solid concrete. Either buy pavers from a building supply store or make a form and pour your own. (See page 17 for more information.)
Above right: This patio, with a floor that looks like stone, was actually formed by laying pieces of broken concrete in a bed of sand.

Finished Surfaces

A broom dragged across wet concrete provides a good non-slip finish. A wood float gives a smoother finish, but one that still provides sure footing when the surface is wet. Use a steel trowel for a slick finish.

Exposed Aggregate

This is a surface covered with small stones scattered while the concrete is still wet but firm enough to support them. Distribute the stones evenly across the surface and embed them using a float until you can just see the tops. When the concrete has hardened (approximately three hours), spray the surface with water and brush off excess concrete to expose the stones. Take care not to dislodge the stones while sweeping.

Traditionally, the rocks used to seed exposed aggregate surfaces are ½ to ¾ inch in diameter. However, the same method can be used to create paving decorated with stones that are much larger. Just make sure that the concrete bed is thick enough to embed the stones.

Etching

It is simple to press a pattern into wet concrete. Using a pointed tool such as a screwdriver, you can draw a flagstone pattern. Or use a stamp to press in a pattern in the same way you would press a cookie cutter into dough.

Adding Color

The best way to color concrete is to add the coloring agent to the concrete mix, either in a mixer or in a wheelbarrow. This way, the color is mixed through the concrete. For large areas, this can be expensive. An alternative is to pour plain concrete to within about one inch of the desired height, then finish with the colored concrete. A third, and less effective, way is to sprinkle the coloring agent over the surface of freshly floated concrete, then refloat. Realize that it is difficult to get an even color.

Concrete Pavers

Laying concrete pavers is as simple as laying brick in sand. In fact, you use the same basic procedure. These pavers are offered in a variety of colors and shapes. They interlock to provide an even surface, are more durable than brick in harsh winter climates, and withstand chipping better than brick.

To lay pavers you need an even and solid slab. Construct a

solid edging to contain the area you are paving, then spread a one- or two-inch layer of sand over the entire area. Arrange pavers according to the manufacturer's directions. Go over the entire area with a plate vibrator (this tool can be rented) to settle the sand and lock pavers tightly together.

Paving Blocks

You will find a variety of concrete paving blocks at your local building supply store. However, if you need a particular size or shape, it is easy to pour your own.

Concrete Forms

Using scrap lumber, make a wooden form with inside dimensions of the size and shape desired for the finished paver. Add small scraps across corners of a square form to create an octagonal paver. Make a hexagonal form by cutting 30 degree miters at each end of 6 equal lengths. (See illustrations.) Use two thicknesses of ¼-inch plywood or bender boards to make circular forms.

Coat inside of form with motor oil so it can be easily removed. Fill form with concrete and smooth the surface. Allow to harden, then cut between concrete and form with a trowel and remove form.

Cover the blocks and allow them to cure for a few days.

Broken Concrete

An inexpensive way to simulate flagstone is to break up an existing concrete slab into stone-sized pieces. This will work as long as the slab is not too thick or reinforced with rebar or wire mesh.

Work a pry bar under one corner of the slab. This action alone may cause the concrete to crack into pieces. If it doesn't, hit the loosened corner with a sledgehammer. Obviously this is not easy work, but it requires no special skill. Maybe the promise of a party will encourage your friends to help.

There are other sources for pieces of broken concrete. Talk to the foreman at a demolition site and he might be happy to get rid of rubble. Look in dumpsters parked outside houses undergoing remodeling.

Cover-Ups

An inexpensive way to turn a dull patio into a Japanese garden is to pour on bagfuls of gravel. Place a special rock, sculpture, or potted plant in one area and carefully rake gravel into waves or swirls around your centerpiece.

Top: A small patio leading from the master bedroom is transformed into a Japanese courtyard garden. The area was covered with gravel, then rocks and large slabs of stone were carefully positioned. Wire-bound bamboo screen encloses the area, making it totally private but still allowing light to filter through.
Above: Handmade rakes keep a stone-covered area looking immaculate. In decomposed granite or very fine gravel, rakes make sharp-edged patterns. Here, in heavier gravel, they create a softer pattern.

Paver Block Forms

To make hexagonal forms, cut 6 equal lengths with 30-degree angles at all ends

To make octagonal forms, nail miter-cut blocks across all 4 corners

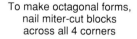

30-degree angles

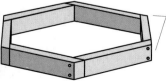

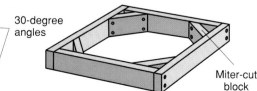

Miter-cut block

WALLS: STRUCTURES THAT DEFINE

In the same way that vertical dividers offer enclosure and privacy indoors, screens, fences, and railings will define your outdoor living space.

Maybe the divider already exists. If so, the following pages will give you ideas on how to heighten or embellish it in order to create a more pleasing or more private outdoor environment. You will also find ways to divide a large deck or patio area into smaller, more intimate spaces.

Realize that in some areas building codes govern setbacks and allowable heights for fences. Always check with your local authorities before you start building.

In the event that you wish to create an outdoor version of a den, turn to page 48, where you will find plans and instructions for building a gazebo. This is a complicated project and one that should not be undertaken lightly.

A fence can be far more interesting than just a boundary marker. Here, an outdoor environment is created by stepped panels that meet behind a small raised deck. The infill consists of 1 by 1s threaded onto a dowel, then endnailed to stringers. (See the section starting on page 24 for help with making the framework.) Between two sections of fence, 4 by 4 beams support a roof structure that offers a feeling of protection rather than actual shelter from the elements.

IDEAS FOR FENCES

Fences serve the simple purpose of marking a boundary. This boundary forms both a physical and a visual interruption by clearly defining limits and creating traffic patterns.

Reasons for Building a Fence

There are many different reasons for building a fence, but the main one is to provide protection and security.

However, fences needn't look like barricades in order to perform their duties—unless you want them to. Low fences or open, lightweight ones can be effective simply because they suggest limits and prompt people to respect them.

The strength of the infill and the height of the fence determine the amount of security and protection you achieve. Choose a style that will give you what you need without imprisoning you.

Another reason for building a fence is to soften the harsh effects of chilling winds, beating rain, glaring sun, and drifting snow.

A fence cannot actually exclude noise unless it is high enough to block sound waves and is sheathed with solid infill on both sides. However, it can insulate you from the annoyance of noise by shielding your perception of it. What takes place outside is unseen; therefore, your awareness of it is minimized.

Above: This interesting infill is composed of alternating boards and bamboo stakes. Notice how bamboo pieces are cut at random lengths taller than the boards.
Opposite: To isolate the patio from the outside world, the owners of this house placed horizontal boards close together on the inside of this framework. This gives the effect of a solid wall around their outdoor living room. However, the top section of the framework is left open to prevent the wall from looking too forbidding from the outside and feeling too imprisoning from the inside.

Types of Fences

When building a fence, you should strive for two things. First, keep it simple. Fancy jogs are distracting (and extra work) unless they serve a purpose.

Second, be generous with space. Tight, stingy spaces make people feel shut in. Even service areas should be large enough for you to move around comfortably.

Once you have decided where your fence will go and how long it will be, you are ready to decide on the style. Following are descriptions of infill—the material that is attached to the stringers.

Board fence is made by facenailing boards to the top and bottom stringers. Although the method is always the same, small changes can dramatically alter the look. Edges of boards can be butted or spaced. Boards can overlap. Boards of different sizes can be mixed and attached in repeating patterns. Boards can be attached diagonally to stringers. Tops of boards can be cut straight, pointed, or scalloped.

Board on board fences are built by nailing boards to both sides of the fence. Boards on one side cover gaps between boards on the other side.

Board-and-batten fences have a dimension that makes them look like solid walls. Boards are first nailed to stringers with only a small expansion gap between. Battens are then nailed over the expansion gaps. Even if the boards shrink as they season, battens conceal gaps, so complete privacy is ensured.

Picket fences conjure up images of fancy-cut tops and special finial frills. These are now hard to find. Lumberyards still carry pickets, but only in limited shapes. You can cut your own tops, of course, but that can be time-consuming. Cabinet shops will do special milling and shaping.

Slats are similar to pickets but narrower. They can generally be purchased by the bundle at lumberyards.

Wire-bound slats are slats woven into heavy wire. This means you can quickly roll out and attach panels.

Lath is a rough-surfaced material, usually about ⅜ inch thick and 1½ inches wide.

Stakes make a handsome, sturdy fence with a rich surface texture. Because they are split, stakes are rough. They are sold at lumberyards by the piece or by the bundle.

Palings (sometimes referred to as stockade fencing) are saplings sharpened to a point at the top and split. They may be difficult to find and they are expensive, but lumberyards will probably be able to order them for you.

Lattice is a classic in the garden. Use lath and make your own or buy prefabricated panels.

Louvers are merely boards set at an angle and endnailed to stringers. To make sure boards are held firmly in place at a consistent angle, groove the stringers before attaching them to posts.

Clapboard fences can be built to match the siding on your house. Attach boards horizontally, starting at the bottom and overlapping each board.

Shingles can be used as infill for a fence as long as you first provide a backing surface such as an existing fence, plywood sheathing, or furring strips.

Wire-bound reed is made from reeds woven with non-corrosive wire. This material is flexible but breaks easily. Durability is not a strong point.

Wire-bound bamboo is similar in appearance to reed fencing but is much stiffer. It is also more durable than reed but is still not recommended for a fence that must last.

Above: Lath screens can be hung on walls in the same way you hang paintings indoors. In addition to covering up a multitude of sins, they can provide support for plants. Opposite: To create the curved top of this fence, it was first necessary to cut a plywood template. Infill follows the line of the template and bender board covers up edges and caps the fence.

In order to erect a fence, a privacy screen, or a windbreak, you must have a sturdy framework to support your structure.

General Techniques

Building a framework for a fence or screen is done in several stages. None of these is complicated, but all should be done carefully so that posts are positioned properly, stand firmly, and are plumb.

The first stage is to plan the position of each post on paper. The second is to mark the position of each post on the ground. The third is to dig a hole for the post. The fourth is to set the posts. And the final stage is to attach the stringers.

Layout

The first thing to do is to carefully work out the layout on paper. Take as long as necessary to ascertain how many posts you will need and where you will need them.

As you make plans, remember that no part of your fence, including the concrete footings, should cross property lines unless you have a written agreement with neighbors. Check the layout with your lot plan.

Once you have your layout on paper, you must clear it with the building department, if required.

Setting Up

In order to tie the string line that will determine the position of each posthole, you must construct batter boards on which to tie a line. You will need a pair of batter boards for each section of a fence line.

To make batter boards, use mason's twine (it doesn't break when stretched taut), stakes, 1 by 3s, box nails, a 50- or 100-feet tape, and a framing square.

Drive a pair of stakes (about 18 inches apart) securely into the earth 2 feet to 4 feet beyond the end of each section of fence. Nail a length of 1 by 3 across outside faces of these stakes.

Stretch a string line between each pair of batter boards. Make sure it is taut. If distance between batter boards is so long that string bows, add a third batter board at midspan and tie a separate line taut between each pair.

Adjust string lines by moving them along batter boards. Make sure they are parallel to the edge of a patio or perpendicular to the wall of a house if that is what you have in mind for the finished fence.

To establish a right angle, use the 3-4-5 triangle measuring technique. Measure 3 feet along one string line and mark the spot with a small flag of tape. Measure 4 feet along the line that should be perpendicular to the first and mark that spot. When diagonal distance between these 2 flags measures 5 feet, string lines are at right angles to one another. For other angles, a simple sight check should be enough.

Marking Posthole Locations

To mark locations for postholes, first measure and mark string line where posts will be placed. Then mark and flag these locations on the ground.

You will need a measuring tape, plumb bob, and masking tape. In addition, have some cloth scraps and long nails, or a can of spray paint, or flour or powdered chalk.

Locations of posts are marked on center, meaning the distance from the center of one post to the center of the next. Since the string line indicates the linear center line of the fence, the exact center point of a corner post is where 2 string lines cross. This is a good place to start measuring for marking posthole locations. Measure along string line and mark each location by wrapping a small flag of masking tape around the line.

Batter Board

3-4-5 Measuring Technique

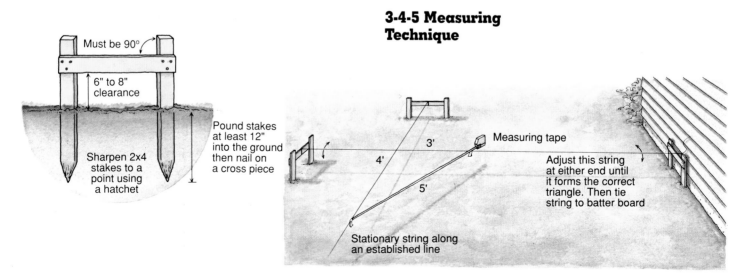

Must be 90°

6" to 8" clearance

Sharpen 2x4 stakes to a point using a hatchet

Pound stakes at least 12" into the ground then nail on a cross piece

3'

4'

5'

Measuring tape

Adjust this string at either end until it forms the correct triangle. Then tie string to batter board

Stationary string along an established line

When all post locations have been marked on string line, use a plumb bob to transfer locations onto the ground. Mark the spot by poking a nail through a scrap of cloth and sticking it into the ground. Or drip a handful of flour or chalk there. Or spray the spot with paint.

When you've got all marks, cut a little V-notch in the batter board where string line now rests. Untie strings but leave batter boards in place. They will guide you when you set and align posts.

Digging Postholes

Now comes the hard part—digging the postholes. There is no special technique for digging postholes, though the aim is to cut a plumb hole with clean, straight sides to suffi-cient depth. If you can under-cut the hole (make it wider at the base than at the top), all the better. This is the best way to anchor the post in the earth. To make the job as easy as possi-ble, choose the proper digging tool for your situation.

If you have only a few holes to dig, a hand tool will be just fine, but don't even consider using a shovel. A shovel cannot give you the clean, straight-sided hole needed to stabilize posts. In rocky soil, a clamshell digger works well, although the double handles tend to break down the sides of the hole if you need to dig much deeper than 2 feet. If the soil is loose and free of rocks, a single-handled earth drill or a bladed scoop digger will work.

When you need to make a lot of holes, consider using a power-driven earth auger that will drill a hole of the correct diameter, or hire a drilling firm to do the work. Posthole dig-ging tools can be rented at tool rental outlets, lumberyards, or hardware stores.

Once all the holes are dug, clean them out so that no loose earth remains. If you are using concrete post footings, remove the diggings. Spread them evenly in surrounding planting beds, or cart them away. If you're using earth-and-gravel backfill footings, keep the soil for the mix.

Shovel about 6 inches of gravel into the bottom of each hole for drainage. A rock in the bottom of each hole makes a solid post foundation. If you have rocks on your site, put one in the bottom of each hole and then add enough gravel to create the 6-inch drain bed.

Digging Tools

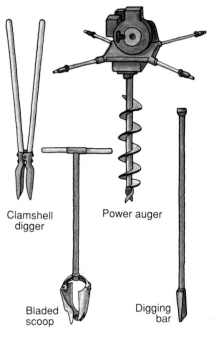

Clamshell digger

Power auger

Bladed scoop

Digging bar

Marking Posthole Locations

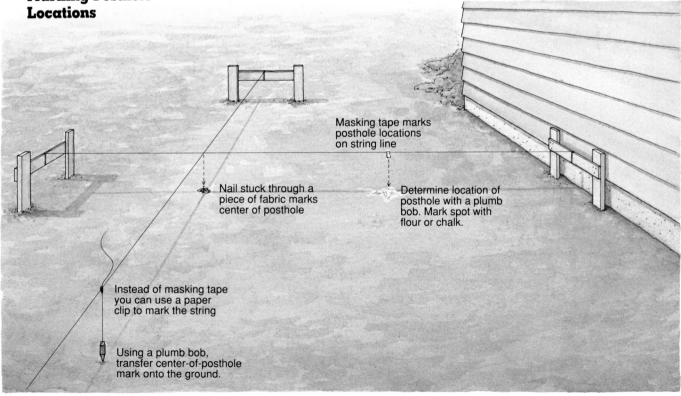

Masking tape marks posthole locations on string line

Nail stuck through a piece of fabric marks center of posthole

Determine location of posthole with a plumb bob. Mark spot with flour or chalk.

Instead of masking tape you can use a paper clip to mark the string

Using a plumb bob, transfer center-of-posthole mark onto the ground.

Erecting Posts

Setting posts is the most critical part of the installation. If they are plumb and in perfect alignment, you'll breeze through the rest of the construction process. The fence will be upright, handsome, straight, and true. If posts aren't plumb or are poorly aligned, you will be forced into a lot of extra fitting and special cutting to coax parts together.

Restretch string lines between batter boards so that they now indicate outside face of fence posts. Measure the actual thickness of end post and divide that measurement in half. The result is the distance that the string line should move away from the V-notch previously made on batter board. Move the line toward outside face of fence.

Place, plumb, and brace end posts in holes. Stand an end post in the hole and twist it about 2 inches into gravel bed. Add a couple of braces (1 by 3 or 1 by 4 boards) about two-thirds of the way up post on 2 adjacent faces. These need to pivot, so use only one nail per brace (a duplex nail is easy to remove later). With a helper, use a level to plumb post on 2 adjacent faces—one person holds the post in position while the other aligns and plumbs it.

When everything is just right, pound a stake firmly into the ground next to bottom of each brace and use a couple of box nails to fasten brace to stake. Repeat this process for other end post.

When both end posts are aligned and braced, stretch another string line about 18 inches below top of posts.

Proceed down the line, placing, aligning, and bracing each successive post, just as you did for end posts. The string lines will help with positioning, but don't let posts touch strings or they will throw off the line. When all posts are braced, set them permanently in footings.

Aligning and Bracing Posts

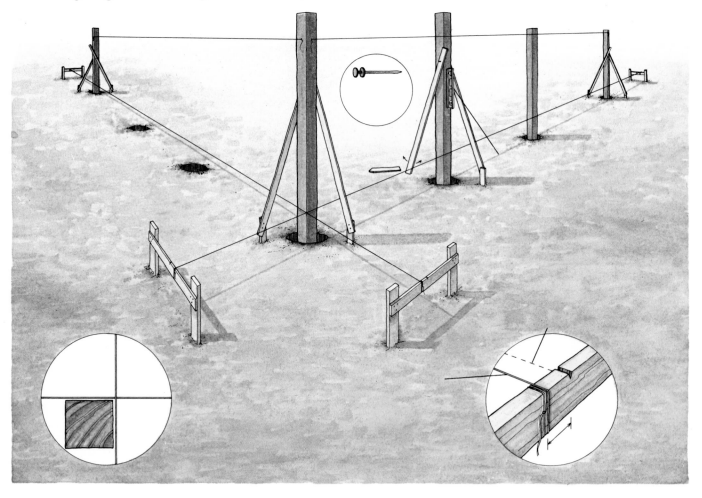

Footings

If what you will be fastening to the post is fairly light and will not be subjected to movement, you can use earth-and-gravel footings. However, posts will be much stronger if the footing is filled with concrete.

Earth-and-Gravel Footings

The key to making posts secure is to tamp each successive layer of backfill vigorously once it's placed in the hole. The best tool to use for this is a shovel handle. It fits easily in the hole and compacts the backfill, and the weight of the shovel blade adds extra heft to each tamping stroke. You can use the end of a 2 by 2 or a 2 by 4 if it's easier for you to manage.

Overfill the hole, sloping it away from the post. This prevents water from gathering around the post and rotting it.

Concrete Footings

Whether you mix your own concrete (1 part cement to 3 parts sand to 5 parts gravel) or buy premixed sacks, the batch should be stiff enough to pack into a ball in your hand. This gives you about 20 minutes before the mix begins to set up. Make sure the bottom 2 inches of post are embedded in gravel before placing concrete in the hole. Shovel concrete in the hole and poke it with a pipe or a broomstick to work out any air pockets. Overfill the hole at the top and slope it away from the post.

Leave braces in place until concrete has set up and cured.

Setting a Post in Gravel

Setting a Post in Concrete

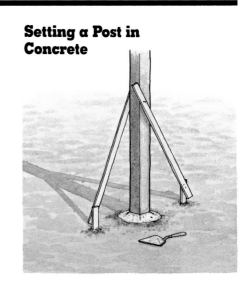

Earth-and-Gravel Backfill

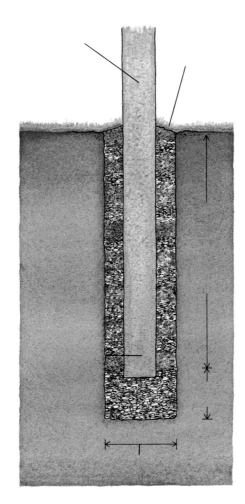

Concrete Footing

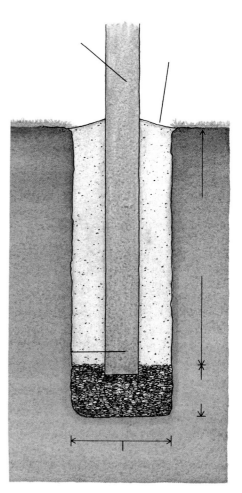

Adding Stringers

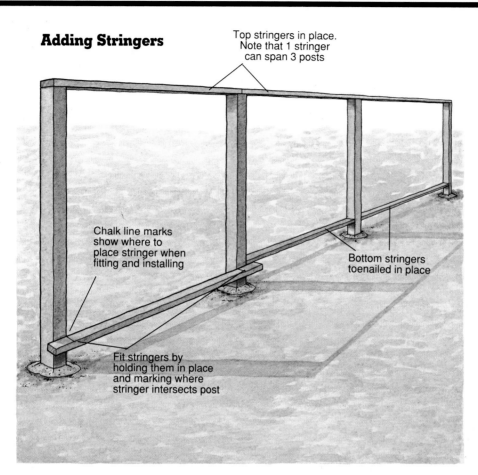

Top stringers in place. Note that 1 stringer can span 3 posts

Chalk line marks show where to place stringer when fitting and installing

Bottom stringers toenailed in place

Fit stringers by holding them in place and marking where stringer intersects post

Nailing

On stringers that overlay posts, either flat or on edge, face nail using 4- or 5-nail pattern

Spanning stringers

5-nail pattern

Top of post

Butting stringers

4-nail pattern

On stringers that butt posts, use a 6-nail pattern. Toenail all nails

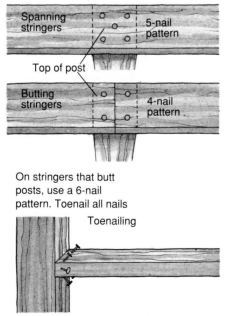

Toenailing

To make nailing easier, start nails in stringer then position stringer and hammer nails all the way in

4-nail pattern

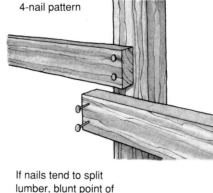

If nails tend to split lumber, blunt point of nail before starting it

Blunting nails

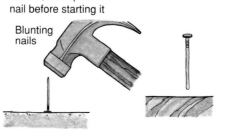

Cutting Posts

In order to measure and mark the posts for cutting height, fasten a nail at that point and secure a chalk line to it. Run the line out to other end post, use a string level to check it, and pull it taut and snap it.

Using a handsaw or a circular saw, cut each post to height.

Adding Stringers

The next job is to turn what is now a row of posts into a framework. You do this by nailing stringers across the posts. These stringers are what the infill is nailed to.

Now it's time to put on your nail belt and fill the pouches. A generous use of nails is the secret to the longevity and appearance of a fence.

Nail top stringers to top of the post. Make sure ends of lengths fall at a post location. Mark and cut top stringers to length and nail them in place.

Before attaching bottom stringers, remove braces if they are in your way. If they're not, leave them; they will add stability to the developing frame. Always measure from top of the posts down.

Mark positions of bottom stringers on each end post and hammer in a nail at these points. Run a chalk line between nails, adjust it for level, then pull it taut and snap it.

Either measure the length of stringer needed with a tape or hold stringer in position and make a line at the point where stringer intersects post.

When frame is complete, strip away any remaining bracing and clean up the debris.

# POST TOPS

Generally, fence posts are cut square, and in many situations, this is appropriate for the style of the fence. However, you can dramatically alter the look of a fence merely by ornamenting the posts.

Embellishments

Following are some of the ways you can ornament fence posts.

Routed Top

Experiment on a scrap piece of wood that matches the dimension of your posts. Try making grooves of various depths. Also change the angle of the sides.

As a finishing touch, cap each top with a square cut from a piece of lumber that is larger than the post. This, too, can be routed with a decorative edge.

Capped Top

This simple change is an appropriate addition to a fence with square lines. It is particularly suitable on a very wide post.

Cut one slice of wood out of the same stock used for the post and another out of smaller stock. Glue and nail the smaller piece to the larger one and attach to the post.

Chamfered Top

Chamfering (beveling) the top of a post gives a finished appearance, and it also causes water to shed off all four sides.

A chamfer can be accomplished with either a plane or a saw, depending on which tool you prefer working with and on how smooth a surface you wish to achieve.

When chamfering a post, you will probably find it simpler to shape all four sides to a point. Either leave the post with a peaked top or cut off the peak to give a flat top. (Illustrations show both versions.)

If you wish to exaggerate the recess, paint or stain the smaller block a dark color before attaching it. This way, it will "disappear."

Angled Top

If you have a circular saw, you can easily cut angled tops on existing fence posts. Work on a firmly planted ladder and set your saw so that the angle will be the same on all posts.

Another method is to add an angled top rather than cutting one. Use a square block of matching post material. Cut it in half diagonally and you will have tops for two posts.

Finials

Look around local lumberyards and in home center stores and you will probably find a variety of finials or pieces that can be used as caps.

The method of attaching the finial on the post will depend on what type you choose. If the finial is specifically made for the purpose, you should have no problem. But if you have chosen an item intended for another use or are combining more than one item, make a mounting plate out of a slice of stock. Attach finial to plate, and then attach plate to post.

Routed Top

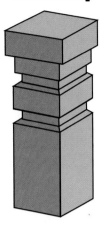

Capped Top

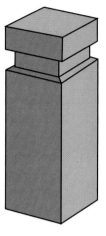

Peaked Chamfer

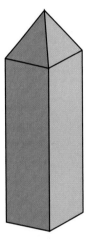

Flat-Topped Chamfer

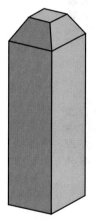

Angled Top

Finial

RETAINING WALLS

Adding a retaining wall is an imaginative way to bridge a change of level between a steep bank and a deck.

Building a Retaining Wall

Hillside lots present special challenges, but when the problems are overcome with shifts of level, the outdoor area is often more interesting than a level piece of ground.

If you have a backyard that consists of a steep slope and a small deck, consider gaining space and creating a planting bed by cutting back the slope and installing a retaining wall.

You may have to obtain a building permit to build a retaining wall, although permits are not usually required for walls three foot high or less. However, even without an inspection, you just can't throw this project together. A retaining wall must be strong. The earth behind the wall exerts tremendous pressure, particularly after heavy rain or snow.

Plan how you will carry water away from the back of the wall. You can install drains or dig a sloped watershed behind the footing ditch and fill it with gravel after the wall is built.

Installing a Footing

First, install a concrete footing on which to erect the wall. If you don't, the wall will soon crack and list.

Dig a footing trench that is twice as wide as the wall and at least 6 inches deep. If you live in an area that gets extreme frosts, extend footing down below frost line.

Build forms by first setting stakes every 18 inches along both sides of trench. Attach form boards to stakes so that lumber is ½ inch above ground. Using 1 by 6 boards for a 6-inch footing or 1 by 8 for 8-inch footing, nail boards to inside faces of stakes. Tie sides of form together with 1 by 2s nailed across at 2 foot intervals.

Reinforce footing and wall with rebar. To determine position for rebar, lay out a run of concrete blocks beside or in footing ditch, carefully spacing them ⅜ inch apart. Mark position and remove blocks. Every 4 feet, place dobies (small concrete piers) to support a horizontal length of rebar, holding it 3 inches above ground level (a code requirement). Wire vertical lengths of L-shaped rebar to horizontal piece avoiding ground contact. Rebar should be long enough to extend through two finished courses of blocks.

Pour footing and screed flush with tops of form boards. Before concrete sets up, make sure upright lengths of rebar are plumb.

Laying Concrete Block

Lay out a dry run of first course. Space blocks ⅜ inch apart and check for level and fit. When satisfied, remove all blocks except 2 end ones.

Spread a layer of mortar on footing. Mortar should be approximately 1 inch thick and about 1 inch wider than the block on both sides. Press end blocks firmly into mortar bed and then stretch a mason's line between end blocks. Use line as a guide but check often with a level, complete first course. Butter one end of each block before pressing it in place.

If you are building a straight wall, the second course (and every alternate one) starts and ends with a half block so that joints overlap. On the third course, you will need to extend rebar. Wire on an extension piece and fill cell with concrete, tamping it to make sure the cell is completely filled.

Check constantly for plumb and level. Set up a mason's line as a guide, or use a long, straight 2 by 4 to make sure your courses are level. As you work, keep scraping excess mortar from joints. As long as it has not hardened, this excess can be reused. Continue until wall is the height you require.

On long walls, 60 feet or more, incorporate expansion joints to prevent wall from cracking. There are several products sold for this purpose, including special tongue-and-groove blocks. Check building supply stores for products that will best suit your purpose.

Concrete block walls are commonly capped with flat concrete blocks, which are simply mortared in place. If you prefer, use flagstone or brick mortared in place. If you wish to install a wood cap, fill cells with mortar, embedding anchor bolts that will secure the wood cap to the wall.

Finishing the Wall

If you dislike the look of a concrete block wall, face it with stucco or cover it with wood.

Stucco Finish

First paint the entire wall with a concrete bonding agent so that the stucco will adhere. Stucco is applied in 2 coats—a scratch coat and a finish coat.

Mix up stucco and trowel on first coat. Press it firmly against wall and smooth to a layer approximately ⅜ inch thick. Before it dries, scratch stucco with a wire brush or broom to roughen surface. (This allows finish coat to bond properly.) Let stucco dry about 48 hours.

Apply finish coat, making it about ⅜ inch thick. Smooth this finish coat or texture it as desired. You can also add a coloring agent to the finish coat.

Cladding With Wood

To face a concrete block wall with wood, first attach nailing cleats. Using a powder-actuated fastening tool, fire fasteners through 2 by 4s into concrete block wall. On the wall shown, boards are positioned horizontally. Therefore, attach vertical nailers spaced 2 foot on center. (If boards are to be vertical, attach horizontal nailers at top and bottom and, if necessary, between these two.)

As facing also forms a backrest, shim bottom of each vertical slightly so that boards will slope backward.

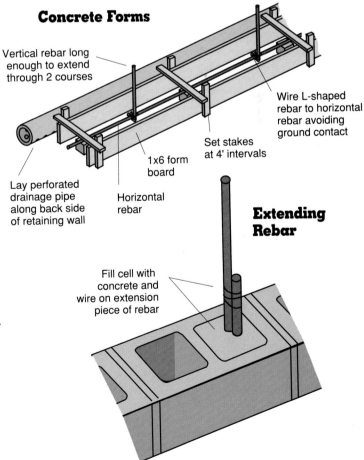

Concrete Forms

Vertical rebar long enough to extend through 2 courses

Wire L-shaped rebar to horizontal rebar avoiding ground contact

Set stakes at 4' intervals

1x6 form board

Lay perforated drainage pipe along back side of retaining wall

Horizontal rebar

Extending Rebar

Fill cell with concrete and wire on extension piece of rebar

RAILINGS

Change the look of a deck with a new railing. These 36-inch-high walls can open up a desirable view, block out an undesirable one, shield you from wind, and provide interesting textures. The same treatments can be used on fences and screens.

Replacing Railings

Not all decks need railings, but for those that do, code requirements will dictate the height (usually 36 inches), maximum distance between rails (between 6 and 9 inches), and lateral strength (15 pounds per lineal foot). Other decisions are up to you.

When a deck is positioned to take advantage of a view, it is a shame to interrupt sight lines with either horizontal or vertical stripes of conventional railings. Solve this problem by replacing rails with wire screen or translucent panels.

If privacy and seclusion are important, the answer is to replace rails with a solid wall or to compromise with a railing that is partially solid but has an opening below the cap rail.

Although solid walls may benefit you by shielding you from the elements and from inquisitive eyes, they can present problems. A solid wall is far more prone to moisture damage because it creates covered spaces where water can accumulate. Take necessary precautions when building by installing moisture barriers and providing air circulation.

Wire Screen

Wire screening, also called welded fabric, comes in rolls of various widths with various mesh dimensions. It may be galvanized or coated with colored vinyl.

If you purchase a dark-colored screen or spray-paint-galvanized material to match a dominant color in your landscape, you will find that the mesh tends to blend into the background.

Attach wire to posts and stringers with galvanized poultry-wire staples. When you start stapling, make sure that the wire strands are perfectly vertical and horizontal. It will be impossible to straighten them later on. Holding each staple in place with needle-nose pliers makes hammering much easier.

Transparent Panels

Glass or plastic panels are another option for a railing that does not interrupt sight lines. Glass must meet code requirements, which generally means using safety plate or tempered glass.

Sheet plastic commonly available is either acrylic, which scratches and even splits fairly easily, or polycarbonate, which is very durable but expensive. Because both of these materials tend to expand and contract a great deal, you should always leave some space around the edges.

Lattice Screen

This type of railing is designed for a deck where you desire some privacy but still want to see out. Lattice is used as an infill to create the obscured area of the railing so that you can still see through. However, any fencing or siding material can be substituted.

Measure an appropriate distance up from the decking boards and down from the cap rail or make these distances conform to code requirements. At these points, attach horizontal rails between posts. Nail lattice panels to these rails or weave your own lattice.

Solid Wall

Solid railings will shield you from unsightly views and wind. They can also visually tie the deck to the house if they are clad in the same siding material.

Depending on the configuration of the existing railing, it may be necessary to add extra vertical nailing posts. These should be firmly attached to the deck joists and cap rail. To alleviate the problem of moisture damage, cover the top of the wall before attaching the cap rail. Use heavy building paper, such as No. 30 felt, or have sheet metal caps made.

On the deck side of the wall, allow space for water to escape and air to circulate between the decking boards and the base of the wall. On the outside face, the cladding can either terminate at deck level or extend down beyond to screen deck support members.

If desired, the capped wall can be topped with a strip of open railing or a custom-welded pipe rail.

Privacy Wall

There are times when a three-foot-high wall does not allow enough privacy. For example, when your deck adjoins your neighbor's. As long as code allows, the solution is to raise the height of at least one part of your railing.

In order to raise the height of the railing, you must also raise the height of the posts. The best way is to replace existing posts with longer ones, anchoring them firmly to deck joists. If this is not feasible, firmly anchor new pieces to existing posts.

Before cladding your new wall, take the opportunity to add exterior lighting. Run wire from under the deck and fasten the box to the new post. Or run wire through posts from the exterior wall of the house.

Wire Screen

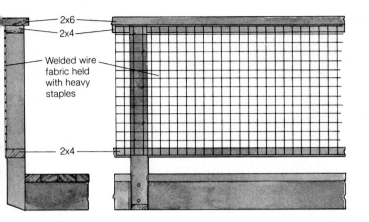

2x6
2x4
Welded wire fabric held with heavy staples
2x4

Transparent Panels

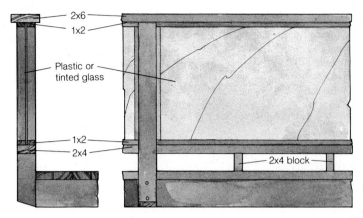

2x6
1x2
Plastic or tinted glass
1x2
2x4
2x4 block

Lattice Screen

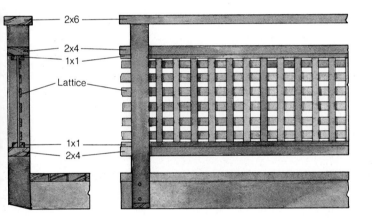

2x6
2x4
1x1
Lattice
1x1
2x4

Solid Wall

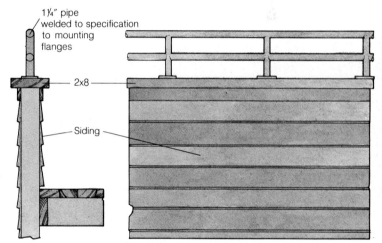

1¼" pipe welded to specification to mounting flanges
2x8
Siding

Privacy Wall

ROOFS: SHELTERS THAT SHADE AND PROTECT

The need for a roof over your head is a basic one. When you are outside, this need is less important psychologically, but there is still something comforting about sheltering under an overhead structure. When the sun is strong, the comfort becomes physical—the shelter provides shade.

In this chapter you will find a variety of structures that can be erected to provide shade and shelter as well as to define your deck or patio. The basic structure is always the same— you need posts to hold it up and a ledger to hold it to the house. You will find framing techniques beginning on page 40.

As long as you provide an adequate support system, you can vary the pattern of beams and rafters. Cross-members can be shaped and stacked at will. Maybe you live in a part of the country where you want dense shade. In this case, clad your framework with closely spaced members. If your structure is merely to define the outdoor space or add patterned shadows, clad the framework with openly spaced members.

Realize that in many areas, erecting an outdoor structure of this kind is governed by building codes. Check with local authorities before you start.

The ledger that supports this overhead structure is attached to posts anchored to siding. An alternative method is to attach the ledger directly to the house. See page 40 for more information.

IDEAS FOR OVERHEAD STRUCTURES

Maybe you need to shade an outdoor area, shield yourself from inquisitive neighbors, add architectural interest to your house, or provide support for climbing plants. You can solve all of these problems with an overhead structure.

Types of Overhead Structures

On the following pages, you will find ideas and projects for building a variety of overhead structures. Although these structures look different, utilize different materials, and serve diverse purposes, the support systems are basically the same. (See page 40 for more on building a structure.)

Shade Structures

The most common reason for building an overhead is to provide shade on a deck or patio that adjoins the house. This might stretch the entire length, or it may just shade a portion of the outdoor area.

Privacy Screen

Even if you are good friends with your neighbors, you may feel uncomfortable knowing that someone upstairs or next door has a clear view of your outdoor relaxation area. An overhead structure will block that view without causing offense.

Architectural Interest

Sometimes an overhead is installed for architectural reasons rather than for shade. When building an overhead that is primarily intended to link outdoor areas to the house, use materials that match those on the exterior of your house. Paint or stain new wood to match and add matching trim.

Arbors

You may wish to install an arbor for any of the reasons mentioned above or merely for training plants.

In many parts of the country, foliage makes an ideal cover. During the summer, when it is desirable to shade an outdoor area and the windows of your home, the leaves on a vine are thick and dense. In winter the leaves fall, allowing the sun to warm the house.

Build arbors to shade your patio or a planter filled with delicate specimens, to dramatize an archway, to soften the lines of entrance, or to conceal a storage area.

Freestanding Structures

An overhead structure does not have to be attached to the house. Maybe you want to protect an outdoor eating or cooking area. Maybe you want to build an enclosure over a hot tub or children's play area.

To build a freestanding structure, you will have to set a minimum of four posts (see page 24), join them with beams, and attach rafters before roofing. (For more information, see page 40.)

Coverings

Materials used for rails and infill can be as open or as solid as desired. What you use will depend on the function of the structure and the form you wish to create.

Wood

Rails can be made from any board lumber intended for exterior use. Commonly, 2 by 4s or 2 by 6s are used for rails laid flat on cross-beams. To resist bowing, or to create a more substantial-looking roof, the rails can be laid on edge. However, realize that this will increase costs. You can use 2 by 2s and 3 by 3s exclusively or in combination with wider boards.

Awning

To add color or to provide deep shade, make an awning to stretch across your structure. The material used must be strong enough to prevent the wind from tearing it, which is why canvas is commonly used. Fasten the canvas securely to the framework with battens nailed along all edges. Or attach grommets to the canvas and lace it to the rafters. Or seam edges of canvas, insert dowel, and fasten dowel to overhead structure.

However you attach the awning, do not make the fastening too permanent. Even a strong canvas will tear, fade, and become water stained, and you will want to replace it.

Awnings can also be made out of parachute silk or mesh fabric, and they do not have to be solid. You might want to consider mounting panels rather than seaming widths of canvas to each other. This is particularly appropriate if you wish to provide deep shape in one area only.

Lattice

Lattice is crossed wood creating a checkerboard pattern. This can be two layers with the second one laid perpendicular to the first, or the second layer can be woven over and under the first.

You can buy lattice as ready-made panels, or you can weave your own. Ready-made panels are time savers and are not expensive. If you plan to use them, make sure you construct your overhead structure based on the size of the panels. The edges must fall in positions where they can be securely fastened to the framework.

If you plan to make your own lattice covering, use slats or lath.

Bamboo

Bamboo is another material that makes an attractive roof covering. Lay and lace individual pieces together or buy ready-made panels and staple them in place.

If you use the thinner type of bamboo shade material, realize that it probably will not last longer than a couple of seasons.

Lath

Rough lath is an inexpensive material for roofing an overhead structure, but it is generally more suitable for a smaller, freestanding structure than for a large one attached to the house.

Above: Posts that support this trellis-covered overhead are built up to look like substantial columns. To imitate this look, build a base for each post. Make a miter-cornered box larger than the post dimensions. (Attach the fourth side after positioning the other three sides around the post.) There will be a gap between the inside face of the box and the post. Therefore, insert spacers before nailing box to post or hold box in place by nailing bottom edge of slanted molding to box and top edge to post. To make the post appear larger, attach plywood panels to each face. Trim with bead molding. It is not difficult to cut out the two pieces that form the pediment. However, it may not be easy to fasten them in place. If the pieces are light, you can nail them. A more secure method is to use lag bolts, countersinking the heads. Paint columns to make all attachments blend into the post.
Left: A simple grid forms interesting patterns on the concrete beneath and shields windows from hot afternoon sun. Brick platforms, serving as seats or plant pedestals, disguise footings for the posts.

Above: A small structure mounted over a planter provides support for climbing plants. Cross-beams are supported by beams attached to both sides of the two posts. These cross-beams could cantilever to either side of the posts, or they could be centered on the post. For more on this, see the project on page 46. Right: The shaped ends of all beams and cross-beams distinguish this shelter. Here, the owner-builder used angle cuts to get the effect he wished to achieve. You could round ends or shape them in any way you please.

Above: A romantic outdoor eating area deserves a special canopy. This intriguing and skillfully executed overhead structure gives diners a sense of protection. Four posts define the area to be covered. Rafters and rails extend different amounts beyond the beams. The screen, suspended from beams, adds a second and lower "ceiling".

Left: Overhead structure is angled to form a passageway leading from the parking area to the front door. Although it doesn't offer any real protection from the elements, it does enclose the space.

FRAMING TECHNIQUES

In order to attach an overhead structure to a house, you must build a support structure similar to the one required for an aboveground deck. You need to set posts, attach beams, and install a ledger before laying on the rails. Techniques for setting posts are described starting on page 24; this section describes the procedures necessary to attach a ledger.

Basic Principles

The basic overhead structure attached to a house is built by fastening a ledger to the house, setting a line of posts along the front edge, linking the posts with beams, and securing rafters (cross-beams) to both ledger and beam. Rails forming the infill are fastened to the rafters.

Ledgers

The ledger (generally a length of pressure-treated 2 by 6) provides a sill on which the rafters of an overhead structure will rest. Therefore, it is extremely important that this member is attached firmly and securely to the house. Anchors holding it in place must be long enough to penetrate through siding and into house framing.

Positioning a Ledger

On a two-story house, you will probable want to mount a ledger at a height that matches the interior floor of the second

story. In this case, drill through the siding and anchor the ledger to floor joists. Find a reference point visible from both inside and outside the house to determine the position of the floor joists. A window is an excellent reference. On the inside, measure the distance from the sill to the floor and add the dimensions of the finished flooring and any subfloor. On the outside wall, measure down this amount from the bottom of the window, allowing for any difference in interior and exterior window trim. Mark this point, which should indicate the top of the interior floor joists or rim joist.

On a single-story house, first make sure that a ledger attached under the eaves will allow enough clearance for rafters and rails and still provide sufficient headroom. Then locate suitable framing members for attaching the ledger. On a single-story house, these will probably be wall studs. If your house is clad in siding, the nailing pattern will indicate the

location of studs. If the exterior is stucco, once again a window makes a handy reference point to determine location of framing members. On a wood-framed house, there should be a cripple stud (a double 2 by 4) on both sides of a window. Determine the center point of the second (outside) stud and you should hit the center of a 2 by 4 at this point and at every 16-inch (sometimes 24-inch) increment. Make marks on the wall where they will not be obscured when you put the ledger in place.

Attaching a Ledger

To build a strong overhead structure, the ledger must be firmly anchored and level. Nail the center of the ledger temporarily in place and brace it at the ends. Check for level and, when satisfied, nail the ends in position.

On a wood-clad house, drill pilot holes and attach the ledger with lag screws. On a masonry wall, insert expansion shields in pilot holes. (This will mean removing the ledger.)

Flashing

Even if you are using pressure-treated lumber, it is a good idea to protect the ledger with flashing. Nail this to the wall above the ledger, caulking around edges. Bend it around the top of the ledger so that it extends a couple of inches down the outside face.

Posts

Spacing of posts depends on the height of the post, the dimension of the post, and the general size of the overhead structure. Refer to the charts on page 43 for guidance.

Attaching Posts

If they will be set into the ground, install posts, following directions on page 24. If posts will be set into a concrete patio, mark positions, dig holes, and pour footings, following directions on page 27. Add pier supports or suitable post anchors.

Before cementing pier supports to concrete footings, soak both with water. Then spread concrete on footing and set pier in place. Check to make sure that the nailing plate is level.

If you are using metal connectors, they must be set into the concrete footing. There are many types of anchors available. Choose ones suitable for the dimension and height of your posts. (See page 42.)

Cutting Posts

The height of the posts depends on how many layers will create the roof of your overhead structure. A basic structure consists of just one layer of rails attached to one layer of rafters. In this case, you will probably cut the posts flush with the top of the beam or rafter.

More complicated roofs are built by attaching at least one more layer of rails on top of the first one. These may be laid directly on top of the first layer or on top of another layer of rafters. If you are planning a multilayered infill, you may want posts to extend as high as or beyond the top layer.

Set the two corner posts temporarily in position. Stretch a mason's line from the top of the ledger to each post and, using a string level, mark the post. Stretch the line between marks on posts and check again. Stretch the line along the top of the footings. If they are level, use corner posts to determine the height of all the posts. If they are not, set all posts temporarily in place and mark them. Remove posts and cut to desired height.

Beams

Size and lengths of the beams depend on spacing of posts. Refer to the charts on page 43.

Depending on your design, bolt the beams to the front and back faces of posts or anchor them to the top of posts. If possible, use single lengths.

Rafters

Refer to the charts for appropriate lumber for the rafters. The weight of the rails and the distance from the ledger to the beam are determining factors.

In many designs, the rafters extend beyond the front face of the posts. And rather than a simple crosscut, you may want a more decorative end. If so, cut the rafters before mounting them. Cut one and use it as a pattern to make all identical. Cuts may be angled, rounded, notched, or any combination that pleases you.

Rails

Now that you have a sturdy structure, top it with rails. This infill can be composed of a variety of material laid in many different ways.

Attaching a Ledger with Lag Bolts

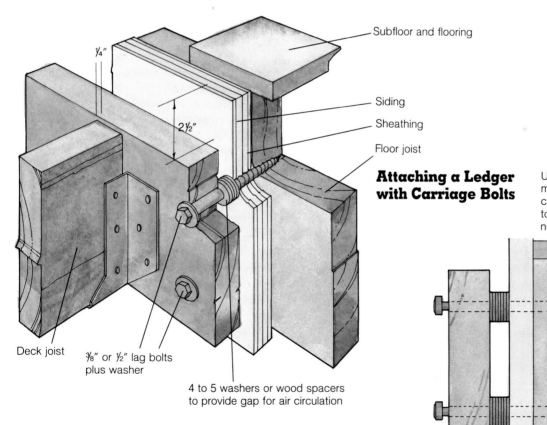

¼"

2½"

Subfloor and flooring

Siding

Sheathing

Floor joist

Deck joist

⅜" or ½" lag bolts plus washer

4 to 5 washers or wood spacers to provide gap for air circulation

Attaching a Ledger with Carriage Bolts

Use carriage bolts or machine bolts if you can get under floor to attach and tighten nuts

Metal Framing Connectors

The strongest way to fasten two framing members together is to use metal framing connectors (often referred to as anchors or hangers). The most commonly used connectors are shown here, but there are dozens of other types.

Joist Hangers

These connectors support cross-beams or rafters that are attached to a beam or ledger. The size varies according to the size of lumber to be held in place—2 by 4s to 2 by 10s. Some varieties will hold 4 by 4s or doubled beams. Forty-five degree hangers or pivoted hangers are also available.

Post Anchors

These connectors anchor posts to concrete piers or slabs. Some are embedded into fresh concrete; others are bolted to an existing slab or to the plate on a concrete pier support.

Post Caps

If your beam or cross-beam will sit on top of posts, attach post caps to hold them in place. Generally, the connectors are one piece, but there are two-piece types made to clamp around posts and beams that are already joined.

T-Strap

This simplified version of a post cap strengthens both sides of a joint. Horizontal arms connect to the beam and the vertical tail connects to the post.

Corner Post Cap

This type of connector looks like half of a standard post cap. It comes in two pieces and is designed to be attached after the beam is in position.

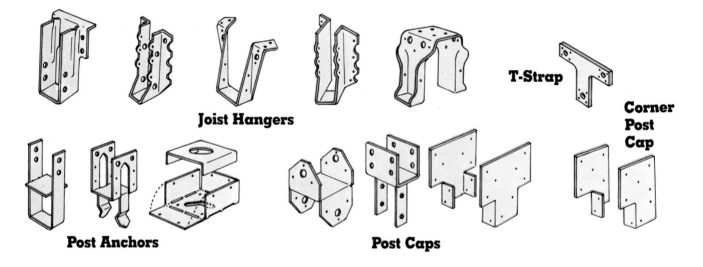

Joist Hangers

T-Strap

Corner Post Cap

Post Anchors

Post Caps

Using Post and Beam Charts

The two charts on the opposite page are included so that you can determine the suitable size, height or length, and spacing of posts and beams.

Some of the projects in this book require setting posts and installing beams. The size and dimension of these pieces is not specified because individual situations, requirements, and preferences determine what will be required to tailor a project to your needs.

Sketch what you are going to build, then consult these charts before finalizing any plans or ordering any lumber.

Beam Spans

Refer to your plan and determine the spacing between beams. If beams are 9 feet 8 inches apart, refer to the column headed 10. This refers to 10 feet. (When your measurement falls between 2 numbers at the top of the columns, always use the higher one.) If you are cutting beams out of lumber belonging to species group 2, you will see that you can use a 3 by 10 for spans up to 6 feet, a 4 by 10 for spans up to 7 feet, and so on.

Minimum Post Sizes

Refer to your plan and determine the spacing between beams and the distance between posts. If the beams are 8 feet 6 inches oc (measured from center of one to center of next) and posts are 11 feet 6 inches apart, multiply these figures. The result—97¾ square feet—is the load area. Therefore, refer to the column headed 108. (When load area amount falls between 2 numbers at the top of the columns, use the higher one.) If you are cutting posts from lumber in species group 3, you will see that you can use a 4 by 4 post up to 6 feet high, a 4 by 6 post up to 8 feet high, and so on.

Beam Spans[1] (Post Spacing)

Species Group[2]	Beam Size (in Inches)	Beam Spacing[3] (Joist Span in Feet) 4	5	6	7	8	9	10	11	12
1	4×6	Up to 6'								
	3×8	Up to 8'		Up to 7'	Up to 6'					
	4×8	Up to 10'	Up to 9'	Up to 8'	Up to 7'	Up to 6'				
	3×10	Up to 11'	Up to 10'	Up to 9'	Up to 8'		Up to 7'		Up to 6'	
	4×10	Up to 12'	Up to 11'	Up to 10'	Up to 9'		Up to 8'		Up to 7'	
	3×12		Up to 12'	Up to 11'	Up to 10'	Up to 9'		Up to 8'		
	4×12			Up to 12'		Up to 11'	Up to 10'		Up to 9'	
	6×10					Up to 12'	Up to 11'	Up to 10'		
2	4×6	Up to 6'								
	3×8	Up to 7'		Up to 6'						
	4×8	Up to 9'	Up to 8'	Up to 7'		Up to 6'				
	3×10	Up to 10'	Up to 9'	Up to 8'	Up to 7'		Up to 6'			
	4×10	Up to 11'	Up to 10'	Up to 9'	Up to 8'		Up to 7'			Up to 6'
	3×12	Up to 12'	Up to 11'	Up to 10'	Up to 9'	Up to 8'		Up to 7'		
	4×12		Up to 12'	Up to 11'	Up to 10'		Up to 9'		Up to 8'	
	6×10			Up to 12'	Up to 11'	Up to 10'	Up to 9'			
3	4×6	Up to 6'								
	3×8	Up to 7'	Up to 6'							
	4×8	Up to 8'	Up to 7'	Up to 6'						
	3×10	Up to 9'	Up to 8'	Up to 7'	Up to 6'					
	4×10	Up to 10'	Up to 9'	Up to 8'		Up to 7'		Up to 6'		
	3×12	Up to 11'	Up to 10'	Up to 9'	Up to 8'	Up to 7'			Up to 6'	
	4×12	Up to 12'	Up to 11'	Up to 10'	Up to 9'		Up to 8'		Up to 7'	
	6×10		Up to 12'	Up to 11'	Up to 10'	Up to 9'		Up to 8'		

[1]Beams are on edge. Spans are center-to-center distances between posts or supports. (Based on 40 psf deck live load plus 10 psf dead load. Grade is No. 2 or better; No. 2 is medium-grain southern pine.)
[2]Group 1—Douglas fir and larch and southern pines; Group 2—Hem fir and Douglas fir south; Group 3—Western pines and cedars, redwood, and spruces.
[3]See Using Post and Beam Charts, opposite.

Minimum Post Sizes[1] (Wood Beam Supports)

Species Group[2]	Post Size (in Inches)	Load Area[3] (Beam Spacing × Post Spacing in Square Feet) 36	48	60	72	84	96	108	120	132	144
1	4×4	Up to 12'				Up to 10'			Up to 8'		
	4×6						Up to 12'			Up to 10'	
	6×6									Up to 12'	
2	4×4	Up to 12'		Up to 10'		Up to 8'					
	4×6			Up to 12'		Up to 10'					
	6×6					Up to 12'					
3	4×4	Up to 12'	Up to 10'	Up to 8'			Up to 6'				
	4×6		Up to 12'	Up to 10'			Up to 8'				
	6×6			Up to 12'							

[1]Based on 40 psf deck live load plus 10 psf dead load; Standard grade 4×4 posts, No. 1, and better for larger sizes.
[2]Group 1—Douglas fir and larch and southern pines; Group 2—Hem fir and Douglas fir south; Group 3—Western pines and cedars, redwood, and spruces.
[3]See Using Post and Beam Charts, opposite.

OVERHEAD TRELLIS

This overhead structure is built to create a
grid of squares that cast straight-line shadows
on the deck beneath. In keeping with the
geometric look, ends of beams and rails are
square cut.

Building the Trellis

Beams and rails on this rectilinear trellis are spaced 12 inches on center. This will provide dappled shade. If you wish deeper shade, fill in the squares with extra rails. Do this over the entire roof or just a part of it. You can also vary the dimension of the squares by spacing beams and rails differently.

Size and spacing of posts depends on the span and strength of the beams. (See charts on page 43 for guidance.)

Materials Required

6×6 posts
1×8 casing to face posts
2×10 for 2 beams
2×6 for cross-beams
2×3 rails for infill

Constructing the Trellis

First, attach a ledger to the house. See page 40 for instructions.

Dig and fill postholes with concrete. See page 27 for instructions. While concrete is wet, set in an anchor large enough to house 1 by 8 casing. Cut posts so that tops will be flush with tops of 2 by 10 beams and face all 4 sides of each post. To do this, it will be necessary to rip-cut 2 pieces of casing for each post to the dimension of 6 by 6 post. Other 2 sides overlap post. (See illustration.) Bolt posts to anchors.

Bolt 2 by 10 beam on each side of each post.

Lay 2 by 6 cross-beams across 2 by 10s. Place them on edge, spaced 16 inches, on center. Toenail to 2 by 10s.

Lay 2 by 3 rails across 2 by 6s, spacing them so that they are 12 inches, on center.

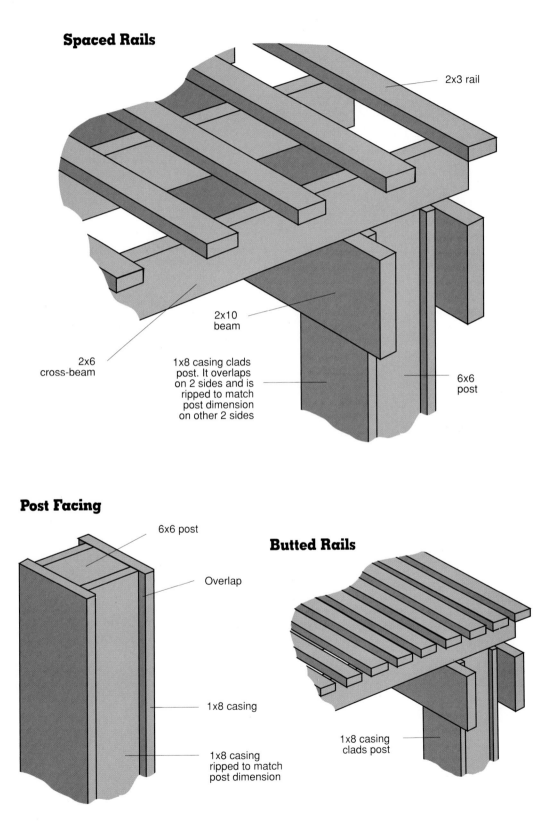

Spaced Rails

2x3 rail

2x10 beam

2x6 cross-beam

1x8 casing clads post. It overlaps on 2 sides and is ripped to match post dimension on other 2 sides

6x6 post

Post Facing

6x6 post

Overlap

1x8 casing

1x8 casing ripped to match post dimension

Butted Rails

1x8 casing clads post

SIMPLE ARBOR

This arbor forms a shelter for a planter. The structure is simple, and if you train a vine to climb up the posts and weave through the slats, you will add color and interest.

Building the Arbor

The support for this arbor is created by attaching 2 by 6 joists to span the distance between 6 by 6 posts. See post sizes and beam span charts on page 43 for appropriate distance between posts or if you wish to alter lumber sizes.

Materials Required

4×6 for posts
2×6 for beams
2×4 for rafters
2×2 for rails

Constructing the Arbor

Set posts in concrete as described on page 27 or bolt them securely to deck support members close to the planter that the arbor will cover.

From the top of the post, measure down a distance equal to the width of the beams plus the width of the rafters. Make a mark to indicate the position of the bottom of the beam. Mark all posts and check for level.

Attach beams on both sides of posts with carriage bolts.

Cut rafters to cantilever an appropriate distance. (They may cantilever from either side or from both sides of the post.) Nail rafters to beams as well as to both sides of post. Add extra rafters wherever needed to improve appearance or to prevent rails from bowing.

You now have the support structure on which to lay the 2 by 2 rails.

ENTRANCE LANAI

Build a roof over the gate in a fence to make a more imposing entrance. Shape ends of all posts, beams, and rafters.

Building the Lanai

Notice that the posts extend beyond the top surface of the lanai and the ends are shaped. For more on shaping posts, see page 29. Also notice that size of lumber decreases as it approaches the top.

Materials Required

2 pairs, 6×6 posts
2 pairs, 3×8 cross-beams
2 pairs, 3×6 beams
6 pairs, 2×5 cross-beams
4 pairs, 2×4 beams
17, 3×3 rails

Constructing the Lanai

Dig and pour concrete footings. (See page 27.) Estimate height and shape tops of posts. Anchor posts to footings.

Cut beams, cross-beams, and rails to desired length, and shape ends as shown or in any manner you wish.

Measure post and make a mark to indicate desired height of first pairs of cross-beams. Bolt 3 by 8s to post at this mark. Using hex bolts and washers, bolt 3 by 8s on both sides of each pair of posts.

Lay 3 by 6s across 3 by 8s. Nail to both sides of each pair of posts.

Lay 2 by 5s across 3 by 6s. Nail pairs to both sides of each pair of posts. Nail other 2 pairs, equally spaced, between them.

Lay 2 by 4s across 2 by 5s and nail pairs to both sides of each pair of posts.

The final layer is a row of 3 by 3s. Lay them across 2 by 4s and nail in place.

VICTORIAN GAZEBO

This gazebo will add another dimension to your outdoor area. It can act as an outdoor den—a place to read or just daydream. It can also serve as a romantic dining room or as just a pretty structure that increases your enjoyment of being outside.

Building the Gazebo

Before ordering or cutting any material, read through the instructions carefully to make sure you have the time and the ability to complete this project: It is not an easy one.

Materials List

All lumber used for in-ground or ground contact should be pressure treated. Where construction practices indicate potential moisture problems, aboveground structural members should also be treated or be cut from a heartwood product of a naturally durable species such as western red cedar. LP-22 indicates treated for ground contact; LP-2 is specified for aboveground use.

Foundation

8 to 12 bags premixed concrete
8, 6×6 post anchors and galvanized nails or bolts
2 precast 14" pier pads
14" stakes

Posts

All treated to ground-contact standards (LP-22)
8, 12' lengths 2×4
16, 12' lengths 2×6
Moisture barrier material (composition shingles, for example)

Beam

2, 9' lengths 2×6 treated for ground contact (LP-22)

Deck Framing

All treated to aboveground standards (LP-2)
6, 10' lengths 2×6
3, 12' lengths 2×6
2, 8' lengths 2×6
4, 10' lengths 2×10

Decking

All treated to aboveground standards (LP-2)
14, 14' lengths 2×6
4, 12' lengths 2×6
4, 10' lengths 2×6
6, 8' lengths 2×6

Rafters

8, 12' lengths 2×6

Center Block

8' length 2×6
Construction adhesive

Collar Ties

8, 10' lengths 2×6

Gusset Plates

2, 12' lengths 2×6

Roof Decking

Use T&G Select
16, 12' lengths 2×6
16, 10' lengths 2×6
30, 8' lengths 2×6

Fascia Board

4, 12' lengths clear 1×3

Roof

2 rolls #15 felt paper
16 bundles cedar shakes
7 bundles hip and ridge shakes
Decorative finial (optional)

Upper Railings

8, 10' lengths 2×4 for top and bottom rails
8, 8' lengths 2×4 for top and bottom plates
9, 8' lengths 1×2 for verticals

Lower Railings

4, 10' lengths 2×4 for cap rail
7, 10' lengths 1×4 for top and bottom plates
4, 10' lengths 1×2 for verticals
7, 10' lengths 1×1 for stops
7, 10' lengths 1×4 for stops
210 lineal feet T&G 1×4 for vertical boards
4, 10' lengths 2×4 for lower rail

Miscellaneous

Note: All nails should be hot-dipped galvanized. Use common (or headed) nails where they will not show and casing nails where they will.
20 lbs 12d casing nails
1 box 12d common nails
5 lbs 8d casing nails
2 lbs 3d finish nails
2 lbs 1" roofing nails
2 lbs shake/shingle nails
8 post anchors
2, 14" pier pads
2 metal joist hangers
3, 16" framing straps

Side View

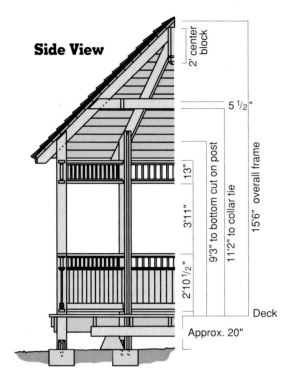

2' center block

5 1/2"

13"

3'11"

9'3" to bottom cut on post

11'2" to collar tie

15'6" overall frame

2'10 1/2"

Deck

Approx. 20"

Exploded View

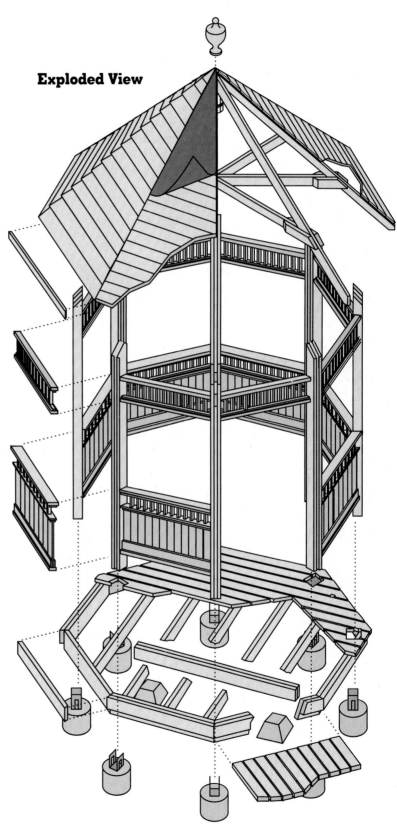

Constructing the Gazebo

Determine a suitable location for the gazebo and mark it out with stakes.

Stakes

Drive a stake (number 1) into center of proposed site. Drive a nail into top of stake and, with a tape or string, make a circle with powdered chalk or lime. Circle has a 6 foot radius.

Decide on location for gazebo entrance and drive a stake (number 2) on a line adjacent to entry opening; place it about 2 feet outside marked circle. Drive a third stake opposite the first so a string tied between them will cross center stake.

Drive 2 more stakes (numbers 4 and 5) at right angles to the first. String a line between stakes, making sure string crosses center stake. (So far, exact length doesn't matter.) To make sure strings are at right angles, use 3-4-5 method illustrated on page 24.

Divide remaining quadrants with stakes and string, as below, to create 8 equal spaces.

Drive a second row of stakes at point where each string crosses the circle. (These should be 6 foot, on center, from stake number 1.) The space between stakes on this inner row should measure 4 feet 6 inches, on center. These stakes need to be exact as they mark centers for each footing.

Footings

Dig a hole for each footing at least 1 foot deep and 15 inches in diameter. Pour footings, making sure they are all at the same level.

Accurately mark point where string crosses circle and install post anchor before concrete sets. Recheck measurements and make adjustments if necessary. Check to make sure all post anchors are level with one another. Use a transit or a long board with a level placed on top. Getting post anchors level and at the correct angle (see illustration) is essential.

Allow concrete to set for 2 days. Recheck measurements and make certain post anchors are all still level.

Posts

Posts are fabricated from pressure-treated lumber. Use two 2 by 6s on the outside with a shorter 2 by 4 sandwiched in the center to support rafters.

Before cutting all sixteen 2 by 6s and eight 2 by 4s required to make 8 posts, make one post as a sample and use as a cutting pattern for others.

Take two 12 feet lengths of 2 by 6 and cut 45 degree angles at one end of each piece. Pieces should measure 11 feet 4½ inches on long side. Pretending it is a rafter, lay scrap length of 2 by 6 across angled end of one post piece. Position a 12' 2 by 4 over top of both so that 2 by 4 is aligned with 2 by 6. Mark angle at top of 2 by 4 and cut. Sandwich and center (side to side) the 2 by 4 between 2 by 6s. Lay scrap 2 by 6 in position. Trim bottom of 2 by 4 flush with bottom of 2 by 6. This is

the first post. Use it as a pattern for the other 7.

Nail posts together, using pairs of 12d casing nails at least every 16 inches on both sides.

Set posts in post anchors, using a composition shingle as a moisture barrier. Shim posts in position, using pressure-treated lumber (anchor will be 1 inch larger than post) and temporarily brace with scrap lumber. Check that posts are 4 feet 6 inches, on center, and 6 feet, on center, from center stake. Distance should not vary by more than ½ inch. Check level at top of posts and adjust if necessary. Using nails or bolts appropriate to the specific post anchor, fasten all posts to post anchors.

Pier Pads

Measure out 3 feet on either side of center stake and set 14-inch pier pads 6 feet apart.

When positioning pier pads, realize that bearing point of pad will be 12½ inches lower than surface of decking.

Installing Posts, Pads, and Center Beam

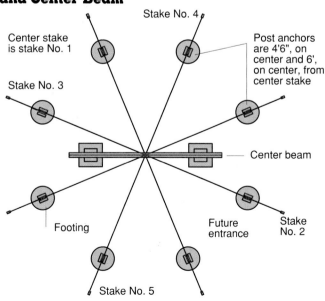

Center stake is stake No. 1
Stake No. 3
Stake No. 4
Post anchors are 4'6", on center and 6', on center, from center stake
Center beam
Footing
Future entrance
Stake No. 2
Stake No. 5

Footing

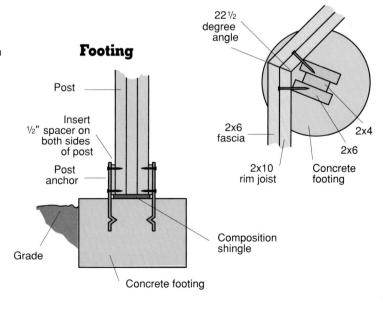

Footing

Post
½" spacer on both sides of post
Post anchor
Grade
Concrete footing

Fascia, Rim Joist, and Post Plan

22½ degree angle
2x6 fascia
2x10 rim joist
2x4
2x6
Concrete footing
Composition shingle

Center Beam

Nail 2 pressure-treated 2 by 6s together to form beam. Lay beam across pier pads so ends are equidistant from center of gazebo. Set a moisture barrier (several composition shingles, for example) between pier and beam. Check beam for level, then toenail to pier support.

Rim Joists

To determine position of 2 by 10 rim joist on posts, temporarily lay a 12 feet to 14 feet 2 by 6 across center beam so both ends of 2 by 6 touch posts. After leveling, mark posts. Mark all posts in this way. Cut 2 by 10 rim joists to length, mitering ends at 22½ degrees. Nail to posts.

Joists and Decking

Cut 5½ inch deck support blocks from 2 by 6 pressure-treated lumber. Predrill and nail blocks to both sides of posts so top is flush with top of 2 by 10. Additional blocking may be required in order to nail decking board securely around posts.

Set 2 by 6 floor joists in place, spaced as shown and flush with top of rim joist. Use joist hangers at both ends of center joist. Endnail remaining joists to rim joist with 12d nails and to posts where possible.

Install 2 by 6 fascia board flush with top of rim joist, mitering ends at 22½ degrees. Use 12d casing nails.

Apply 2 by 6 decking to floor joists, allowing about ½ inch space between boards. (A 12d nail makes a good spacer.) Fit decking around posts and trim ends of boards to a consistent 1 inch overhang.

Upper Post Construction

Post and Rafter Relationship

Fascia, Rim Joist and Post Plant

Deck Framing

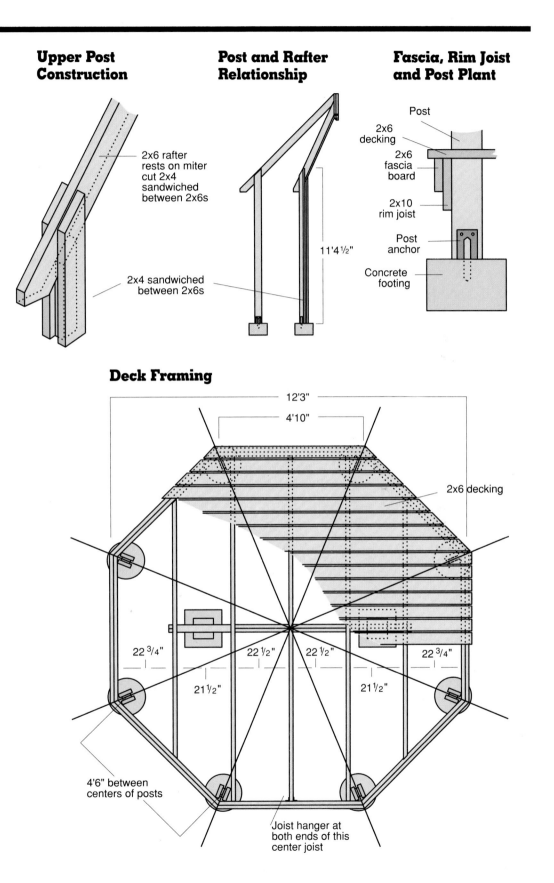

2x6 rafter rests on miter cut 2x4 sandwiched between 2x6s

2x4 sandwiched between 2x6s

11'4½"

Post
2x6 decking
2x6 fascia board
2x10 rim joist
Post anchor
Concrete footing

12'3"
4'10"
2x6 decking
22 3/4"
22 ½"
22 ½"
22 3/4"
21½"
21½"
4'6" between centers of posts
Joist hanger at both ends of this center joist

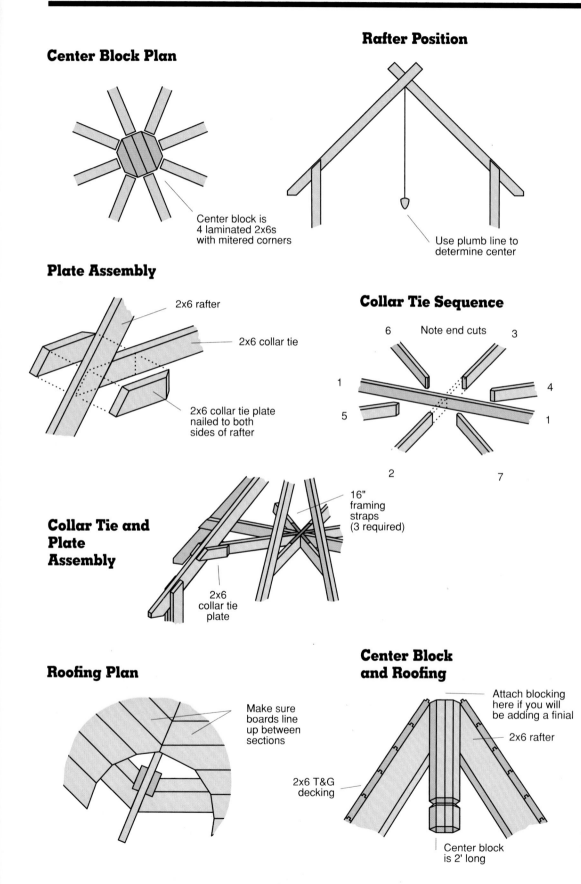

Center Block Plan

Center block is 4 laminated 2x6s with mitered corners

Plate Assembly

2x6 rafter

2x6 collar tie

2x6 collar tie plate nailed to both sides of rafter

Collar Tie and Plate Assembly

16" framing straps (3 required)

2x6 collar tie plate

Roofing Plan

Make sure boards line up between sections

Rafter Position

Use plumb line to determine center

Collar Tie Sequence

6   Note end cuts   3

1

5

4

1

2   7

Center Block and Roofing

Attach blocking here if you will be adding a finial

2x6 rafter

2x6 T&G decking

Center block is 2' long

Center Block

Cut four 2-feet lengths of 2 by 6. Glue and nail these together to form a 6 inch-wide block. Trim and notch as shown.

Rafters

Place 2 opposing 12 feet 2 by 6 rafters in position as shown. Use a plumbline to find the center and tack rafters together temporarily.

Mark position for center block, allowing for 12-inch overhang. Cut 45 degree angles on ends adjoining center block and trim overhanging end as shown. Use this piece as a pattern to cut remaining 6 rafters. (Refer to illustration showing how rafters attach; for now, attach only the first 2.)

Temporarily toenail 2 opposing rafters to center block. Position on posts and check fit. Remove from posts, predrill holes, and toenail first 2 rafters to center block.

Refer to illustration to see how collar tie system fits together. Position 8-foot 2 by 6 collar tie across first 2 rafters. Mark angles for trimming ends. (Piece should measure about 7 feet 4½ inches on long side of angle cut.) Trim and toenail collar tie into position.

Cut two 2 by 6 collar tie plates as shown. Notice that one end is mitered at 45 degrees to match rafter angle; the other end is beveled. Use as pattern for remaining 14 plates (16 plates required for 8 ties).

Nail first 2 plates into position, using 12d nails.

Set roof truss on posts making sure center block is centered and overhang is equal. Nail rafter to post through outer 2 by 6s, using 12d casing nails. Temporarily brace upper part of posts to keep dimensions rigid and true.

Anchor remaining rafters to center block and posts. Toenail to center block; nail to posts.

Following sequence shown, cut remaining collar ties and assemble. Toenail into position.

If you will be adding a finial to the peak, attach pieces of blocking between center block and underside of roof peak.

Install remaining collar plates as shown. Install three 16-inch framing straps as shown.

Collar Rafter Plan

Start first course of tongue-and-groove roof decking flush with ends of rafters, tongue side up and face side down where it will be seen from below. Miter one end of board and allow a little extra length at other end. Facenail first board to rafters.

For remaining boards, cut and miter as before. Attach, using two 12d nails per rafter: one toenailed through tongue and one facenailed. After each triangular section is complete, snap a chalk line down center of rafter and trim other end of decking.

Make sure boards line up between sections to produce coursing effect of grooves.

Roofing Plan

Apply 1 by 3 face trim to end of rafters. Position it flush with top of decking. Miter ends.

Apply roofing paper according to manufacturer's directions, taking care to seal well around peak.

Apply shakes according to standard roofing methods. If desired, install decorative finial on peak. Nail to previously installed blocking.

Upper Railings

Upper railing sections are installed in all 8 bays. Before cutting horizontal boards, measure each opening to adjust for any variation in width.

Cut horizontal 1 by 2s and 2 by 4s to length, mitering ends of 2 by 4s at 22½ degrees.

Each bay requires 12 vertical 1 by 2s, each 8½ inches long. Endnail vertical 1 by 2s to horizontal 1 by 2 rails at top and bottom, 3¾ inches, on center. Using 6d casing nails, nail rail section to 2 by 4 base and cap.

Toenail completed railing section to posts, using 12d casing nails. Build identical rail sections for remaining 7 bays.

Tip: Temporarily nail a scrap of 2 by 4 to posts at a height of 6 feet 11 inches. Blocks will hold completed railing in place while you nail.

Lower Railings

Because there is no railing on entrance bay, you will need 7 sections. As with upper railings, measure each opening before cutting boards.

Cut horizontal members to length, mitering ends at 22½ degrees. Toenail 2 by 4 bottom rail to posts, 1½ inches above deck boards with inside 1 by 4 stop nailed to 2 by 4 with 12d casing nails.

Endnail 1 by 2 verticals to top and bottom 1 by 4s, 3¾ inches on center. Toenail to post 24 inches above bottom 2 by 4.

For each section of rail, cut 14 1 by 4 tongue-and-groove boards to 23⅞ inches and 12 1 by 2s to 6¾ inches.

Assemble 1 by 4 verticals on a flat surface, using a straight edge to keep edges square. Trim last 1 by 4 to size. Using 3d finish nails, temporarily nail 1 by 4 bottom stops and 1 by 1 top stops in place on the panel and check section for fit. Once fitted, secure in position with 6d casing nails.

Build 6 more railing sections for remaining bays.

Access

Build entrance platforms or steps to suit your site.

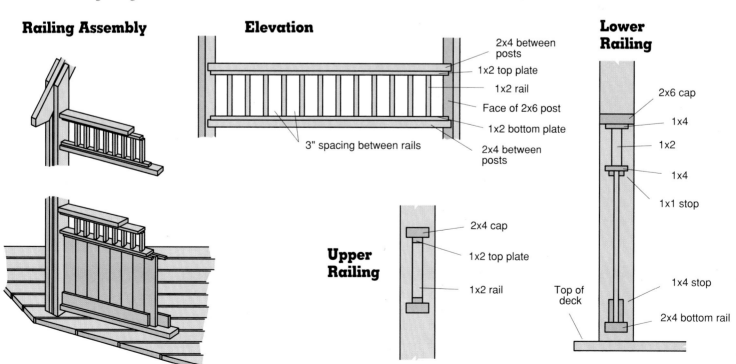

Railing Assembly

Elevation

2x4 between posts
1x2 top plate
1x2 rail
Face of 2x6 post
1x2 bottom plate
2x4 between posts
3" spacing between rails

Upper Railing

2x4 cap
1x2 top plate
1x2 rail

Lower Railing

2x6 cap
1x4
1x2
1x4
1x1 stop
1x4 stop
Top of deck
2x4 bottom rail

FURNISHINGS: ACCESSORIES THAT ADD COMFORT

You have a well-planned space; you have a pleasing effect; but if you don't have somewhere comfortable to sit and enjoy it, you don't have a functioning deck or patio.

If it is necessary to drag out a table every time you feel like enjoying a snack outdoors, chances are that you won't do it. And if you have to go to the garage and pull out chairs on which to sit, it's likely you'll end up indoors. Outdoor furniture should be able to withstand reasonable weather conditions.

Aim to furnish your deck or patio with pieces that allow you to wander outside and sit quietly enjoying a book or watching the children at play. Install seating in many different areas so that you can always enjoy the sunshine (or shade). Seating doesn't have to mean chairs. Low benches (see pages 70 to 73), wide planter rims, and shallow steps all provide perches.

While considering furnishings for your outdoor space, don't forget about feathered friends. Providing feeding stations and houses for birds (see pages 84 and 85) will add immeasurably to your outdoor pleasure.

This outdoor kitchen is for people who are serious about entertaining outdoors. Not only does this unit provide lots of storage, it is equipped with a sink and running water.

IDEAS FOR FURNISHINGS

Furnishing a deck or patio requires the same amount of thought as decorating an indoor sitting room. Provide comfortable places to sit and lounge. Supply the chef with counters and serving tables. Think about lighting schemes. And plan for entertaining a crowd.

Decorating Outdoor Space

Before you buy or arrange outdoor furniture, spend some time watching the way the sun moves across your outdoor living room. (Obviously this varies according to the time of year.) Also notice the direction of prevailing winds. A sunny, protected corner of a patio can be warm enough to enjoy on a mild winter day. If you don't have such a spot, consider building a windbreak in order to create one.

Be generous with whatever space you have. Don't cram all the furniture in one area. Create several sitting areas rather than one large one. This way, people can move around easily and choose to sit either in or out of the sun.

Designate a shelf or closet in the garage or a protected place that will accommodate cushions. It is annoying to find that you can't enjoy a quick break in the sunshine just because seat cushions have been rained on or are wet with morning dew. If you don't have a handy storage place, consider the cart on page 80. It is called a barbecue cart, but it could easily house several cushions. The bench on page 70 is another project that can be adapted to serve as cushion storage. The seat can be hinged along the back edge and the cavity beneath lined with plastic.

Make sure you provide plenty of tables and benches for picnics and barbecues. Position the barbecue where smoke will blow away from your entertaining area, but don't totally isolate it. Outdoor entertaining is casual, and helping or advising the chef is part of the fun of a cookout. Provide lots of surfaces for stacking raw ingredients, basting sauces, and cooking tools.

Artificial light brings an entirely new dimension to the enjoyment of a deck or patio. You don't have to wait for Christmas to string lights in the trees. Run wire up the trunk and illuminate the tree with a galaxy of small, twinkling lights. (Be sure to use strings of lights rated for outdoor use.) Then you can sit outside on a warm evening or relax inside, enjoying a view of the outdoors, on a cool one. Although, you may not be able to connect the wiring for an outdoor lighting system yourself, you can save a lot of money by doing all the planning, digging, and laying of wire. (See pages 60 to 63.)

Above: If you are going to cook outside, an exterior counter is as important as the one in your indoor kitchen. Not only do you require a surface on which to prepare food, you need somewhere handy to store charcoal, dishes, and cooking tools. Because wood is hard to keep clean, the owners chose to cover their counter with tile.

Opposite: Decks are not always attached to the house. Here, a boat dock is furnished with benches, planters, and a lamp post. See page 64 for a differently designed lamp that you can make.

Above: When furnishing a deck, realize that the primary aim is to provide an area in which you can comfortably enjoy being outside. If you have a view as spectacular as this one, it is not necessary to add decoration. Bear in mind that, from indoors, anything placed between the windows and the railing will block the view. In order to avoid loading the deck with lots of furniture, the owners of this home incorporated a bench along one edge. A pipe rail mounted to the cap continues the line of the rail across the front and brings the height of the bench up to code requirements. Opposite: On a deck that is low to the ground, railings can double as benches. However, if your deck is further from the ground than this one, building codes may insist on a higher railing. Typically codes require a deck more than 30 inches from ground level to be surrounded by a railing that is 36 to 42 inches high.

INSTALLING OUTDOOR LIGHTING

Even if you are not a skilled electrician, you can do most of the work necessary to install a lighting system. However, it is advisable to have a licensed electrician check your work and connect the system to the power source.

120-Volt Versus 12-Volt

The main differences between 120-volt and 12-volt (low-voltage) lighting installations are how deep the cable must be buried, the permits needed for the work, the conduit used, and the complexity of the work.

A standard-voltage system is usually more expensive than a low-voltage system and involves a lot more work to install. However, standard-voltage systems light your garden more brightly.

Installing 120-Volt Lighting

Begin by getting a building permit if it is required in your area. This will probably involve taking your final plan to the building inspection office. You may be asked to make changes in the plan so that it conforms to the local electrical code, or to demonstrate that you are proficient enough to do your own work. The inspector will tell you at which points during the installation your work must be inspected.

Materials Required

From your final plan, list the parts you need.

Conduit

Decide whether you'll use rigid PVC or rigid metal conduit. (Your inspector may have already made this choice for you.)

Metal conduit is harder to work with and may corrode in time, but it is more resistant to accidental damage and rodents and can be buried in a shallower trench.

PVC conduit is lightweight and easy to work with and will not corrode. In most locations it must be buried at least 18 inches deep.

Figure out how much conduit you need and add 10 percent as a margin for error.

Boxes

You'll need one outdoor box for each fixture, receptacle, and switch. The only exceptions are boxes for those switches that will be located indoors. These can be standard interior boxes. If you plan to control any lights from 2 separate switches, remember to order extra boxes for this. For wet locations, or to place boxes at ground level beneath fixtures, you can order special junction boxes made of cast iron.

Receptacles

Install outdoor receptacles only in boxes rated for outdoor use. Be certain that these and all outdoor boxes are installed at least 12 inches aboveground, unless they are special cast-iron boxes designed for below-grade installation. The first receptacle on an outdoor circuit should be a GFI receptacle unless the circuit is protected by a GFI circuit breaker installed at the service panel.

Wire

Local codes govern the type of wire that must be used.

Type UF cable can be directly buried in most areas. Type TW or THHN wire must be enclosed in conduit, and you need to combine individual hot, neutral, and grounding wires. Get 2-wire UF cable with a ground wire for general use, 3-wire cable with ground for wiring 3-way switches.

Fittings

You will need couplings to join conduit, boxes, and fixtures together (slip-type couplings for PVC conduit, threaded metal or compression couplings for metal conduit). You will also need threaded PVC fittings for attaching PVC conduit to boxes. Join metal conduit to boxes with insulated bushings. (Do not use set-screw couplings; they are not waterproof.)

Get sweep bends for making 90-degree bends in PVC; do not use smaller fittings sold for water pipe.

Wire Connectors

The best connector for outdoor wiring is a wire nut. Be sure to buy the right size for the wire size you're using.

Time Clock

A time clock allows you to program when and for how long, the lighting is turned on.

Sensors

Power to lighting systems can be controlled by sensing devices. Some of these devices have photocells (which are widely used on city streetlights). Others have infrared sensors that turn on the lights when the infrared beam is interrupted.

Other Materials

You will need 12-inch stakes for marking fixture locations, lime or flour for marking runs, electricians' tape, solvent glue for PVC conduit, concrete blocks and concrete for anchoring fixtures and receptacles, a narrow roll of plastic sheeting to line trenches, caulking compound for sealing holes, and hardware for mounting boxes.

Tools

In addition to tools normally found in a workshop, you will need to rent or buy fish tape for pulling cable through conduit, a conduit bender, a threader for threading pipe ends, and a voltage tester.

Layout

Working from your plan, use wooden stakes to mark locations of fixtures, receptacles, and switches. Then, beginning at the point where each circuit will connect to the power source, mark wire runs on ground by dribbling lime or flour from your hand.

If you are connecting to an existing circuit, the power source may be an existing outdoor receptacle or a switch that is wired directly from the source. If you are installing new circuits, make trenches running to the location of the existing or new panel. Make lines as straight as possible. If the trench must go around an obstruction, plan a gradual curve rather than a sharp bend.

Digging Trenches

Prepare areas where you will be digging trenches: Cut and roll up sod and lift out small shrubs and perennials. To go under a path or walkway, trench close to each edge of the path and drive an iron pipe under it with a sledgehammer. Pull out the pipe and push conduit or cable through the hole, or rent a drill with an earth-boring bit.

Dig trenches at least 4 inches wide and as deep as necessary. Line with plastic.

Assembling Conduit

Cut metal conduit with a hacksaw, smooth cut ends with a file, and thread ends where necessary. (Full-length pieces come threaded at both ends, and pieces attaching to compression couplings don't need threads.) Bend conduit as necessary, avoiding sharp curves that will make it difficult to pull cable through.

Cut PVC conduit with a hacksaw and paint the inside of the fitting and outside end of the pipe with solvent. Twist on fitting and push in place. Work quickly; solvent sets up in just a few seconds.

Assemble conduit adding junction boxes and boxes for outdoor receptacles while making connections. Lay assembled conduit in trenches.

Where an upright section of conduit leads to an above-ground box, widen the trench, slip a concrete block over upright conduit, and set block in the bottom of the trench. (After you have installed and checked the system, you will fill the block with concrete to anchor fixtures.) If you are using PVC conduit or unenclosed UF cable, add a sleeve of steel conduit over the section that will extend aboveground.

Threading Wire

Run wire from power source (without connecting it) to switches that will control that circuit. Leave several feet of wire at the source to make the connection. If switches are indoors, choose a route that causes the least damage—through an unfinished basement, for example. Run a cable from the power source to the location of each switch, then add pigtails (short pieces of wire or cable) to extend to next switch on circuit. From each switch, run a second cable out to lighting fixtures and receptacles that will be controlled by the switch.

Pull cable through previously assembled conduit. (The best tool for this is a fish tape,

Top: Mark lines for wire runs by letting lime or flour dribble through your fingers.
Above: If you use metal conduit, you will need to rent a conduit bender such as the one shown here. Threading wire through smooth, gradual bends is much easier than trying to force it around sharp corners.
Left: Wire, housed in conduit, runs from power source to individual fixtures.

which can be rented at a tool rental store.) Cut the cable at each box, leaving several inches to make connection. At fixture end, leave ample cable to make the connection.

Connecting Wire

At this point, you can hire an electrician to make the connections. This is highly recommended if any of the wiring is around water. The risks of poor wiring are too great to do this work yourself unless you are a skilled electrician. If you feel confident to do the work yourself, continue as follows.

Connecting Switches

Begin wiring at each switch box. Strip cable and attach it to box with the built-in clamps or snap connector. If the power runs from the source through the switch box to lights, use white wires as neutral and splice them together in the box.

For single pole switches, connect one terminal to power-source wire and other terminal to wire going to lights. Splice all ground wires together. If the box is metallic, add a 6-inch pigtail in the splice and connect to box with a screw or approved grounding clip. Mount switch and apply face plate.

Connecting Receptacles

Connect receptacles as you would indoor ones. An end-of-the-run receptacle will be connected only to 2 incoming wires, a middle-of-the-run receptacle to 2 incoming wires and 2 that continue to next receptacle or fixture. The first receptacle on an outdoor circuit should be a GFI receptacle unless the circuit is protected by a GFI circuit breaker at service panel.

Connecting Fixtures

At each middle-of-the-run connection, the junction box should have 2 threaded holes for incoming and outgoing conduit and 1 threaded hole in the top in which the fixture is usually mounted. The box for each end-of-the run fixture will have only 2 holes: 1 for conduit and wire coming in, the other for the fixture.

Wire fixtures according to manufacturer's directions and screw on box cover being sure to include waterproof gasket.

Always point open end of wire nut downward after tightening to prevent water from collecting and corroding the connection.

Connecting System to Source

If your system will not be inspected by the building department, have it checked by an electrician to make sure that conduit or cable is buried to the correct depth and that all connections are sound.

When the system has been approved, have an electrician connect it to the power source. If you do the work yourself, be sure to follow proper safety precautions. Turn off the power before making the connection and check that it is off with a voltage tester.

Testing the System

Turn on switches one by one to make sure all fixtures work. If you find one that doesn't, try replacing the bulb. If this doesn't solve the problem, turn off the power and check with a voltage tester to be sure it is off. Then check connections and the switch itself with a continuity tester. Also check position and angles of fixtures. This is best done at night when you can see the light.

In the end, if everything is where you want it to be, you can fill blocks that support fixtures with concrete. If not, make changes before you fill the trenches and clean up.

Installing 12-Volt Lighting

You don't usually need permits and inspections to install a 12-volt lighting system. If, however, you are installing new circuits to operate a large low-voltage system, or a new GFI receptacle to plug in a transformer, check with the building inspector.

Despite its relative safety, 12-volt lighting can be hazardous if poorly installed. Loose connections or too many fixtures on a circuit can cause heat buildup, resulting in a fire. Follow manufacturer's instructions carefully when running cable and connecting fixtures.

Maximum Length of Wire Run on Lighting Circuits[1]

Total Watts[2]	Maximum Wire Run (in Feet)[3]			Fuse of Breaker Rating (in Amps)
	#14 Wire	#12 Wire	#10 Wire	
100	820	1,370	2,190	15 or 20
200	410	685	1,095	15 or 20
500	165	275	440	15 or 20
800	100	170	270	15 or 20
1,200	70	115	185	15 or 20
1,500	55	90	145	15 or 20
1,800	45	75	120	20

[1]This table applies only to 120-volt lighting systems. For 12-volt systems, follow the manufacturer's recommendations regarding wire size and length of wire runs.

[2]The maximum wire runs are assuming the total load is at the end of the circuit. When the load is distributed over the length of the circuit, the total length can be greatly increased before noticeable dimming of lamps occurs.

[3]Length of wire run refers to distance from the circuit box to the light fixture at the end of the circuit.

Materials Required

Materials for low-voltage lighting may be hard to find. Although some hardware stores stock basic materials and systems in kit form, it may be necessary to order your system.

Cable

Low-voltage cable is usually 2-conductor, direct-burial cable in sizes 12, 14, or even 16. Follow manufacturer's recommendations for maximum length of wire runs.

Connectors

Some systems come with their own clamp-on terminals, which you can plug in without having to cut the cable. Other fixtures are connected with wire nuts, which are usually supplied with them.

Switches and Receptacles

Order any outdoor 120-volt receptacles you need to power your transformers. These should either be GFI receptacles or be installed on a circuit protected by a GFI.

Whether your transformer will be plugged into a receptacle on a 120-volt circuit or wired directly into the circuit, it should be controlled from indoors by a switch. This can be a standard wall switch or a time clock.

Fixtures

Most fixtures will be set into the ground on spikes or hung in trees, but for special situations you can order some with a deck or patio mount.

Fixtures are usually sold complete with bulbs, but you may be able to specify the type or color. Check the manufacturer's catalog.

Transformers

Low-voltage transformers can operate up to several hundred watts, but you may want to divide larger systems among several transformers. Order your transformer for indoor or outdoor installation; indoor ones are less expensive but some require wiring in a fuse.

Most transformers have 2 screw connections for low-voltage cable. You can order multiple terminals in order to make several wire runs from the same transformer as long as you do not exceed the maximum voltage recommended.

Time Clocks

If the time clock is a separate unit, you plug the clock into a standard receptacle and the transformer into a receptacle built into the clock.

Most time clocks can operate only one lighting system. Therefore, all lights will go on and off at the same time unless you wire different parts of the system to different clocks.

Other Materials

You will need 12-inch wooden marker stakes, lime or flour for marking runs, and narrow plastic sheeting for lining trenches. Other than these supplies, there are no special tools required. All you will need are a selection of pliers and screwdrivers and some gardening tools for digging slit trenches.

Layout

Choose a location for the transformer. It can be indoors in a garage or closet, or outdoors. It should be central to lighting fixtures so that wire runs extend out like spokes of a wheel. This will keep wire runs as short as possible.

Mark locations of fixtures with stakes and mark cable runs by dribbling lime or flour out of your hand. Wherever possible, follow natural barriers in the landscape and path edges to protect wire from accidental damage. Do not make wire runs longer than the maximum length recommended by the manufacturer. If you must exceed maximum length, use a larger wire size or 2 cables wired parallel. Contact manufacturer for assistance.

Running the Cable

You can safely lay low-voltage lighting cable right on ground surface, but your yard will look better and the cable will be better protected if it is hidden a few inches below ground.

Starting at transformer end, make a narrow slit trench, 6 inches deep, along line you marked. Line trench with plastic and drop in cable. Leave about 1 foot for connecting to transformer and a loop above ground at each stake marking location of fixtures. Run cable into trees if fixtures will be installed there.

Connecting the Fixtures

It is important to connect fixtures to cable before plugging in transformer. Otherwise, expect to blow the transformer fuse or trip its circuit breaker.

Some fixtures connect with simple clamp-on connectors, which eliminate the need to cut the cable. Others require conventional connections.

Make connections above ground and protect them from moisture by enclosing them in the stems of fixtures or sealing them in epoxy packets available from electrical distributors. If a connection must be made in an underground location, seal it in an epoxy packet.

Installing the Transformer

The transformer should be either wired directly to an indoor switch or connected to a GFI-protected receptacle that is operated by an indoor switch.

Attach low-voltage cables from wire runs, and plug in transformer.

Testing the System

Testing is best done at night when you can see the lighting effect. With the fixtures turned on, check each for proper placement and angle. One advantage of low-voltage systems is that it is easy for you to relocate fixtures if you wish.

If any fixture does not go on, check the bulb first. If it is good, turn off the transformer and check the connection. If all fixtures work but those at the end of the line are dim, check the length of the cable run to see that it doesn't exceed the recommended length. If it does, the dimness is being caused by voltage drop and can be remedied by rearranging wire runs.

LAMPPOST

Light will add to your enjoyment of evenings outdoors in the cool of the night. Make a series of these post lamps to ring a patio, line a deck, or glow around planters.

Building the Lamp

To make this lamp, you must be able to rip and bevel-cut lengths of board. Therefore, it is not advisable to attempt this project unless you have an adjustable circular saw, a table saw, or a radial arm saw.

Louvers can be made from ¼-inch exterior plywood. In this case, you will need to cut ¼-inch wide dadoes (slots) in 1 by 4 frames. Instead of plywood louvers, you can create interesting effects by using sheets of copper or galvanized metal. The metal will catch the light and provide extra sparkle. A single saw cut will provide enough of a groove to house metal louvers.

The post may be cut to any length. For low-level lighting around a patio, a 9- to 10-inch post is high enough. You will probably want to make a higher post for lamps planted in flower beds.

The removable cap allows easy access to the lamp.

Use pressure-treated lumber for in-ground or ground-contact applications. In areas where there are moisture problems, aboveground structural members should also be treated or be made of heartwood of a durable species. Brush or dip cut ends of treated lumber in preservative.

Materials List

Post:
2 lengths 2×6
2 lengths 2×4 ripped to 2½" wide
Louvered sides:
8, 24" lengths 1×4
36, ¼" louvers 3"×6"
Roof:
4, 7" lengths 1×6
Nailers:
4, 5 ½" lengths 1×3
Trim:
4, 16" lengths 1×3
4, 32" lengths 2×2
Cap:
1, 7" square cut from 2×8
Cap base:
1, 5½" square cut from 1×6

Electrical conduit approved for outdoor use
Porcelain socket approved for outdoor use

Constructing the Lamp

Determine length of post by subtracting 15 inches from total desired height. Sandwich 2½-inch pieces between 2 by 6s as shown. Glue and nail together.

Post is held in place on a concrete footing. Dig a post-hole, fill with concrete, and set in a metal anchor. Or set in a purchased concrete footing complete with anchor. (See page 27 for information on concrete footings.)

Thread electrical conduit through center of post assembly and install porcelain light socket on top.

Each one of the 8 side pieces must be dadoed to accept the louvers. Spacing them 2 inches apart, cut 9 dadoes in each 24-inch 1 by 4. Cut dadoes at a 40 degree angle. For a good appearance, make sure dadoes are identical on all pieces. If using plywood louvers, cut dadoes ¼ inch wide by ¼ inch deep; for metal louvers, make a single saw cut ¼ inch deep.

Cut top of 1 by 4s at a 40 degree angle, 2 inches above top dado. Miter edge where 1 by 4s will meet in the corner. (See illustration.)

Miter back edges of 1 by 6 roof pieces to match sides. Glue and nail each roof to a pair of 1 by 4 sides. (Make sure dadoed sides face each other on inside faces of assemblies.)

On inside face of side pieces, measure 4½ inches up from bottom edge and endnail 1 by 3 nailer flush with back edge. Attach nailers to other 3 louver assemblies.

Attach louver assemblies by positioning nailers flush with top of post and nailing or screwing them in place. Apply glue to miters on outside face of sides as you install assemblies.

Now you are ready to add trim pieces. Horizontal trim is made from 16-inch lengths of 1 by 3. Cut 2 notches in each piece so distance between inside edges of notches matches width of your post (approximately 5½ inches). Glue, notch, and nail pieces to post 2½ inches below bottom edges of dadoed side pieces.

Vertical trim is made out of 32-inch lengths of 2 by 2. Position each piece tightly into a corner so that it extends 1 inch above tops of side pieces.

Chamfer 7-inch square cap so that water drains in all 4 directions. Center and attach 5½-inch square to underside.

Glue louvers in place, setting them ⅜ inch away from front edge of dado cut.

Turn on power, screw bulb in socket, and position cap.

Dadoed Side Piece

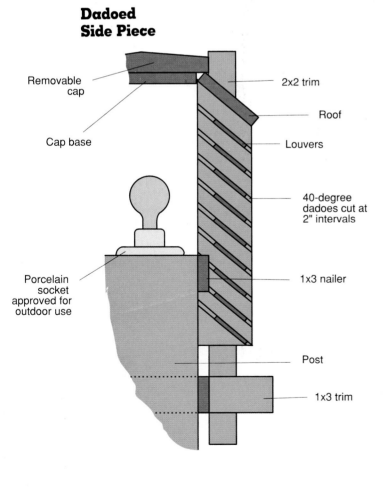

Removable cap

Cap base

Porcelain socket approved for outdoor use

2x2 trim

Roof

Louvers

40-degree dadoes cut at 2" intervals

1x3 nailer

Post

1x3 trim

Top View

2x2 trim

Louvers

1x3 nailer

Dadoed sides mitered to meet at corners

Horizontal Trim

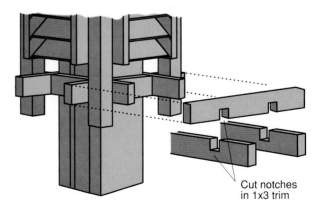

Cut notches in 1x3 trim

PLYWOOD DECK CHAIRS

This ingenuous design allows you to make two deck chairs from just one half of a piece of plywood. A series of saw kerfs makes shaping the rounded arms simple.

Making the Deck Chairs

These chairs can be made as shown or you can make a solid-arm version by adding inserts. You have to cut the inserts in either case. For the open-arm version, inserts are made out of scrap plywood and used as templates to be removed after glue in the frame has dried. For a solid-arm chair, cut inserts out of a second half-sheet of plywood that matches material used for the rest of the sections.

The chairs can be finished as desired, but they will look particularly attractive finished in bright-colored acrylic paint. If you decide to paint your pieces, be sure to prepare them first with a stain-resistant primer compatible with the paint you will be using.

Materials List

4×4 sheet ⅝″ A-B or A-C exterior plywood
Scrap sheet of 4×4 plywood for 2 templates or 4×8 sheet instead of 4×4 listed above

Constructing the Deck Chairs

Mark 4 foot square of plywood following layouts shown. Use a straightedge and a carpenter's square to accurately divide the sheet in half and draw all parts on plywood. Use a compass to draw rounded corners. Be sure to allow for saw kerfs between sections that abut.

To get clean cuts on edges that will show, always cut plywood on the appropriate face. If hand-sawing, use a 10- to 15-point crosscut saw and place panel front face up. If using a hand-held power saw, use a

Panel Layout

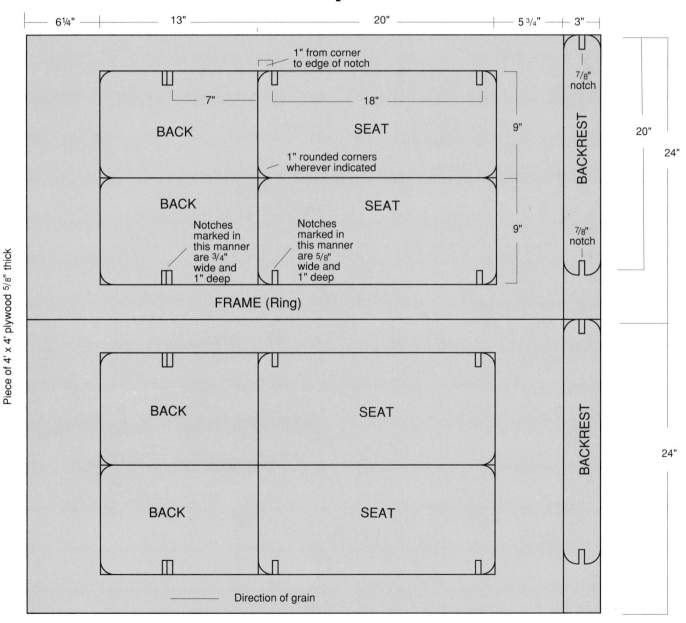

Chair Frame

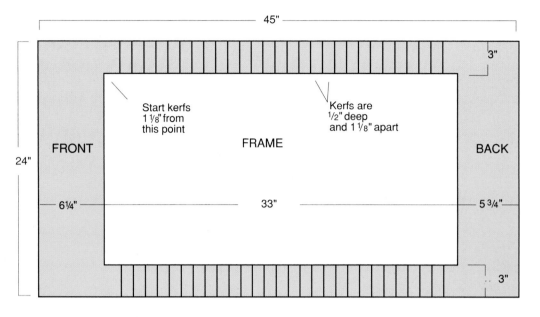

45"

3"

Start kerfs 1 1/8" from this point

Kerfs are 1/2" deep and 1 1/8" apart

FRONT

FRAME

BACK

24"

6 1/4"

33"

5 3/4"

3"

Seat

Backrest

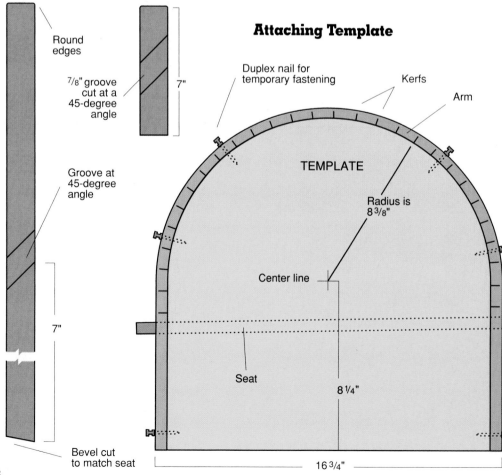

Round edges

7/8" groove cut at a 45-degree angle

7"

Groove at 45-degree angle

Attaching Template

Duplex nail for temporary fastening

Kerfs

Arm

TEMPLATE

Radius is 8 3/8"

Center line

7"

Seat

8 1/4"

Bevel cut to match seat

16 3/4"

plywood or combination blade and place panel front face down. If using a table saw, place panel front face up. To reduce splintering on the back side, clamp or tack a piece of scrap lumber under the cutting line. Use a fine-tooth saber saw for rounded corners and cutting slots.

Before making any cuts, note that plywood surrounding seat and back pieces comprises chair frame. This is a continuous ring. Do not start cuts at edge of plywood.

Cut out chair backs and seats using a circular saw, stopping just short of corners of pieces. Cut rounded corners using a saber saw.

Cut notches at front edges of seat sections. Cut notches in back and backrest sections at a 45 degree angle.

Bevel bottom of backrest pieces so that they rest flush against seat. Also bevel inside corners of backrest pieces so that they lie flush against back.

Before cutting kerfs that allow you to curve arm pieces, apply masking tape to help prevent splintering. The tape should run along edge where saw will exit. Using a circular saw, cut 1/2-inch kerfs spaced 1 1/8 inches apart. (See illustration.)

Using a ruler, straightedge, and compass, measure and mark scrap plywood to use as a template for shaping frames. Rub edges of templates with wax so that you will be able to remove them easily after glue in the arms has dried. For added strength, templates may be permanently installed by gluing and nailing them to frames. If you will be doing this, cut them out of extra piece of purchased plywood.

Fill kerf cuts with glue. Position templates on both sides and gently pull ends toward each other.

Glue and nail seat pieces in place notching them into frame as shown. If you will be removing them, tack templates to frame with duplex nails that are easy to remove when glue is dry.

When glue is completely dry, remove templates and, from the underside, screw chair back to seat. Nail backrest in place with 2d finishing nails.

Countersink screw heads, fill nail holes, sand smooth, and finish deck chair as desired.

Top Views

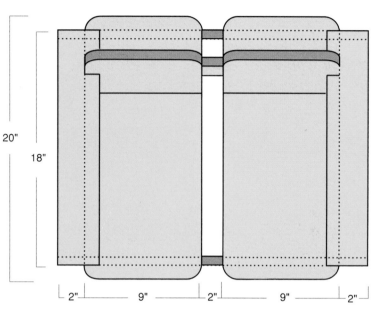

Side View

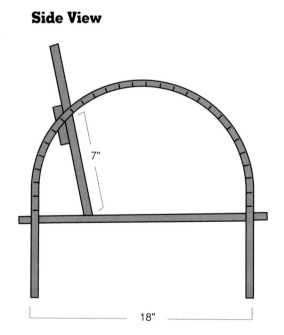

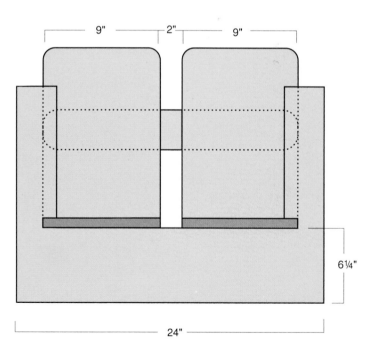

ATTACHED BENCH

This bench, shown on the front cover of this book, is attached to a wood-faced retaining wall. It serves three different functions. First, it offers lots of seating or a spot to stretch out in the sun. Second, it acts as a visual transition between the wall and the deck. And third, it provides a step from which you can reach plants at the front of the sloped bed.

Making the Bench

On a bench of this length, it is a good idea to slope the seat slightly. Not only will this make it more comfortable to sit on, but it will prevent the bench from looking too boxy.

All dimensions are easy to adapt, but these directions are for building a bench that is 16 inches high at the front, 15½ inches at the back, and approximately 16 inches deep. The length is left up to you.

To build the retaining wall and backrest, see page 31.

Materials List

For each leg:
1, 16" length 2×4
1, 15½" length 2×4
2, 14" lengths 2×4
For seat: 3 lengths 2×6 times length of seat
For facing: 3 lengths 1×3 times length of seat

Constructing the Bench

First, build leg assemblies to which the seat will be attached. Plan on positioning legs every 3 feet to 4 feet. (Distance depends on strength of the lumber used for seat. If boards are placed on edge, 4-foot spacing of legs is sufficient. If boards are placed on face, space legs 3 feet apart.)

Nail leg assemblies together as shown, making sure ends are flush. Using a rasp or plane, smooth off corners so top of assembly is flush.

Attach back (shorter length) of leg assembly at appropriate intervals. (See note above.) Use a powder-actuated fastening tool for attaching to a masonry wall. Make sure leg is exactly perpendicular to back wall, then predrill front leg and toe-nail to deck.

Lay 2 by 6 seat boards across legs, leaving a gap approximately ⅜ inch at the back and between each board.

If the bench is so long that you need to use more than one length of board, cut pieces so that ends will fall at a leg. Nail all pieces to each leg.

Using 1 by 6s, nail front facing to front of each leg. If lengths must be joined, cut pieces so that ends fall at a leg.

Bench Planking

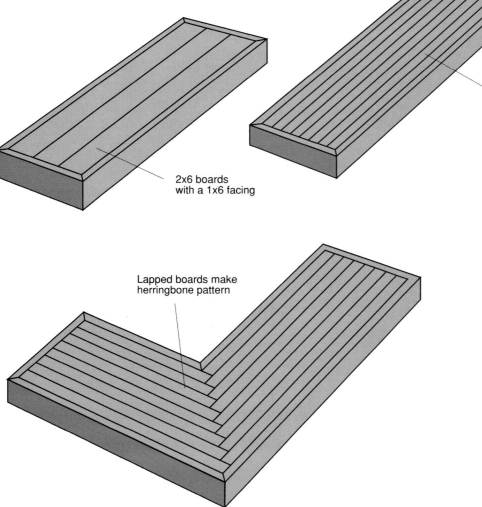

2x6 boards
with a 1x6 facing

2x4 boards laid
on edge or 2x2s
with 2x4 facing

Lapped boards make
herringbone pattern

Leg Assembly

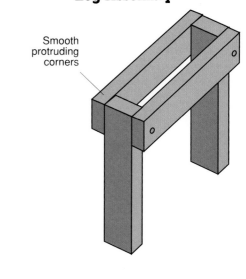

Smooth
protruding
corners

BUTCHER-BLOCK BENCHES

Benches are essential and versatile pieces of furniture on a deck or patio. They can be used for seating, for tables, or as shelves on which to display potted plants.

Making a Legged Bench

Butcher-block tops of this redwood bench can be nail-laminated using economical common-grade redwood. Legs should be made out of construction heart for increased decay resistance.

It is important to get the edges flush when laminating boards together although slight variations can be smoothed with a belt sander. To keep pieces even and level, work on a flat surface assembling the bench on edge. Predrill nail holes to prevent splitting.

The bench is built entirely with redwood 2 by 4s and can be made to any height or length that suits. Directions are to make a bench that is 15 inches wide, 4 feet long, and 18 inches high.

Materials List

Actual dimensions of lumber vary. You may need to make slight adjustments on pieces that must fit exactly. Measure your project before cutting lumber.

8, 4' lengths 2×4 for top
2, 41" lengths 2×4 for top
4, 18" lengths 2×4 for legs
4, 14½" lengths 2×4 for legs

Constructing a Legged Bench

Legs are composed of one 18-inch piece and one 14½-inch piece nailed together so that one end is flush and a seat board fits exactly into notch at other end. Using 8d nails, nail through longer piece into shorter one so that nail heads will not show on outer face. Make 4 leg assemblies.

Lay one 4-foot length on a flat, even surface. Position a leg assembly, notched side down, at either end. Lay one 41-inch length between legs. Nail all to first board in a zigzag pattern, making sure all top edges are flush. Use 12d nails positioned about every 6 inches. Lay another 4-foot length on top and nail as before. Continue until there is only one 4-foot length remaining. Place other 2 leg assemblies on top of bench assembly, notched side up. Lay in second 41-inch length and nail as before. Complete bench by nailing on final 4-foot length.

Smooth bench seat with a belt sander.

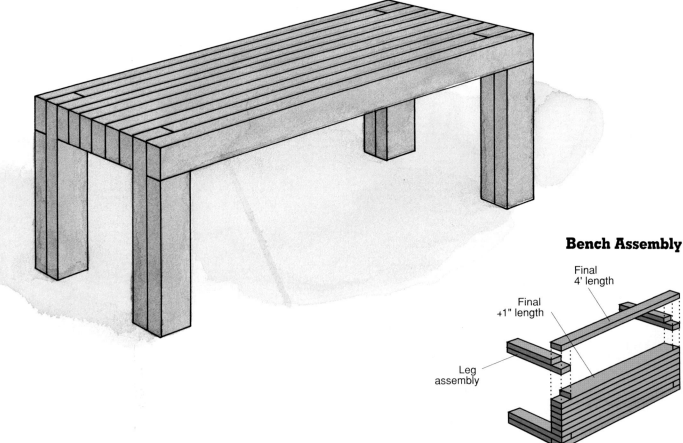

Bench Assembly

Final 4' length

Final +1" length

Leg assembly

72

Making a Solid-End Bench

This bench is made out of the same materials as the legged version. The difference is that the ends are solid and the pieces are glued together and held firm with threaded rod.

Like the legged version, this bench can be made to any length and height. Because of the solid ends, it can also be made a lot wider. Directions are to make a bench that is 4 feet long, 16½ inches wide, and 14½ inches high.

Materials List

6, 4' lengths 2×4 for top
5, 41" lengths 2×4 for top
10, 14½" lengths 2×4 for ends
12, 11" lengths 2×4 for ends
⅜" dia ×15" threaded rod
4 nuts and washers

Constructing a Solid-End Bench

Cut all pieces to length and drill a ⅜-inch hole at one end of a 14½-inch piece. Hole should be centered (1½ inches from each edge) and 1½ inches from end. Use this piece as a guide to drill tops of all 14½-inch pieces and both ends of all 4-foot pieces. It is essential that all rod holes match. On two 4-foot lengths, make ¾-inch countersink holes.

Ends are alternating 14½-inch and 11-inch pieces.

Nail a short and a long piece together so that one end is flush and a seat board fits exactly into notch at other end. Make 8 end assemblies. On at least 2, nail through longer piece into shorter one. This way, heads will not show on outer face.

Insert rod into one of the countersunk lengths. Thread on washers and tighten nuts. Lay length (rod facing up) on a flat, even surface and spread it with glue. Thread end assemblies at either end, notched side down. (Use assemblies without nail heads on front face.) Lay a 41-inch length between. Thread a second 4-foot length

onto rod and spread with glue. Position 2 more end assemblies with a 41-inch length between. Continue in this way spreading glue between each board until only the second countersunk length remains.

In order to avoid nails on the outside face of last end piece, make 2 leg assemblies composed of a 14½-inch length sandwiched between two 11-inch lengths. Nail through longer piece into shorter one that will face front. Nail through second short piece into pair already joined. Position last 2 end assemblies and lay final 4-foot length in position.

Slip washers on rods, tighten nuts, clamp bench, and allow glue to dry. When glue is completely dry, sand or plane surfaces smooth.

Nailing Front Leg Assembly

Front face

73

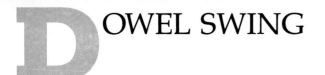 OWEL SWING

Gentle, rhythmic movement provides peace and relaxation. Inside, you head for a rocking chair. Outside, it could be this swing that lulls you into enjoying a lazy afternoon.

Making the Swing

First you will have to find an appropriate place from which to hang your swing. A tree with a sturdy branch is the most obvious location, but you could also suspend the swing from hooks screwed into an overhead structural member.

There are no hard edges on this swing. The entire assembly is made from large dowel, more commonly referred to as closet pole. This is widely available at lumber and home center stores. Although generally made of pine, closet pole is also available in redwood.

The 23¾-inch width of this swing is designed to allow for the most economical use of closet pole, which comes in lengths in two-foot increments. You can vary this width by cutting longer pieces. And you can also add extra pieces to adjust the height and depth of the swing. Work out the most economical length, making sure that you will be able to transport the pieces.

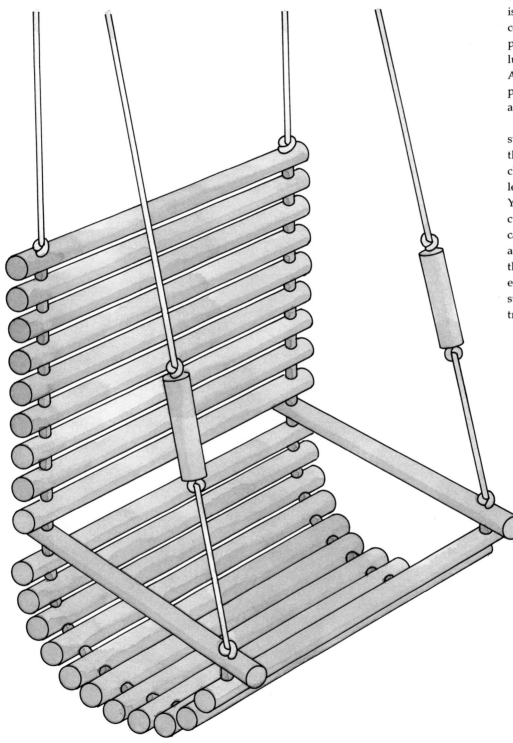

Materials List

20, 23¾" lengths 1½" closet pole
2, 20" lengths 1½" closet pole
2, 6" lengths 1½" closet pole
Scrap piece of garden hose
⅝" nylon rope
Scrap lumber for drilling jig

Constructing the Swing

In order for the swing to hang properly and go together easily, it is extremely important that holes at both ends of each piece of dowel are drilled in matching positions and at matching angles. It is also important that holes are drilled exactly the same distance from ends of dowels. (It would be very difficult to keep track of left and right ends.)

The only way to be sure of accuracy is to build a jig and mark each piece of dowel before drilling it. This might seem a lot of trouble, but it will ensure easy assembly.

Drilling the Dowels

The jig shown is for drilling 1½-inch closet pole with holes 1½ inches from ends. If you are using a different size dowel, adjust accordingly. To ensure that holes will be uniform, mark each length of dowel. Working on a flat surface, hold piece of dowel against a straight piece of ¾-inch stock. Draw a line across entire length of dowel so holes will be at same angle at both ends.

Make a 4-sided jig like the one shown and mark a centerline on top piece, extending it down front edge. Drill a pilot hole through top piece. Insert

dowel into jig, pushing it firmly against the back. Match up center marks on jig with line marked on dowel and drill a pilot hole.

Grip dowels firmly while enlarging holes to ⅝ inch in diameter or make a second jig. Sand off marks on dowel and smooth ends and holes.

Spacers

Spacers are placed between each length of dowel. Either buy a short length of garden hose or use a discarded piece from which to cut spacers. Cut hose into ½-inch long pieces with a sharp knife dipped frequently in hot water, or use a fine-tooth saw blade.

Assembling the Swing

Cut 2 lengths of nylon rope. Each length should be long enough to reach to and from hook or branch that will support swing. Allow enough rope to reach support, then tie an overhand knot. Starting with what will be top of back support, thread drilled dowels and spacers as shown. Remember to add arm supports in appropriate locations. Tie another knot at top of front edge of arm support. Allow 16 inches (less if swing will be used by a child), tie a knot, and thread on hand grip. Knot above grip.

Lash appropriate fittings to ends of rope or tie ends securely to branch of tree.

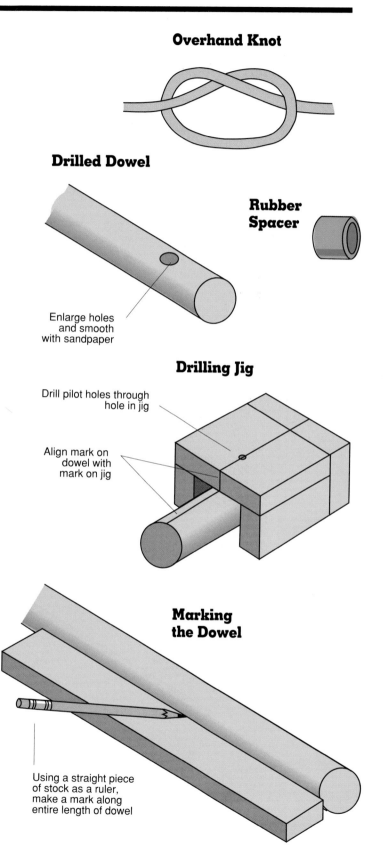

Overhand Knot

Drilled Dowel

Rubber Spacer

Enlarge holes and smooth with sandpaper

Drilling Jig

Drill pilot holes through hole in jig

Align mark on dowel with mark on jig

Marking the Dowel

Using a straight piece of stock as a ruler, make a mark along entire length of dowel

DINING TABLE

Enjoy meals al fresco around this sturdy yet good–looking dining table. The size and height are easy to adjust to suit your space.

Building a Table

Eating outdoors is a joy, but it will become a pain unless the dining area is convenient to a food-preparation center. This might be outside the kitchen door or close to the barbecue.

The table should be high enough to sit at, but it can be lower than the standard indoor dining table height, which is 29 inches. You will be using outdoor chairs and benches around this table, and they are usually lower than standard dining chairs. Measure your chairs and make sure your table will be comfortable to sit around. Directions are for making a table that is 44 inches wide, 62 inches long, and 26 inches high.

The top of the table shown is made with boards that are 5¼ inches wide (actual size). If your boards are different, adjust the length, the number of boards used, or the space between boards. Position boards approximately ⅜ inch apart.

Because all pieces butt, it is very important that all cuts are completely square. Get your lumberyard to cut pieces if your saw cannot accept 4 by 4s.

To make this table, you will have to drill right through the 4 by 4s and into the members that support them. This requires a long bit. You will also need to drill ½-inch holes deep enough to countersink the heads of the lag screws. The designer of this table felt that the heads added an interesting pattern. If you disagree, you can drill a deeper countersink and plug the holes.

To avoid hitting your knees on sharp edges, shape ends of 2 by 4 rails. The simplest way is to miter-cut the ends, but you could round off corners or cut a stepped pattern.

Materials List

4, 24½" lengths 4×4 for legs
2, 25" lengths 4×4 for lower
leg supports
2, 25" lengths 2×4 for upper
leg supports
1, 41" length 2×4 for stretcher
2, 60" miter-cut lengths 2×4
for rails
9, 44" lengths 2×6 for top
58, 5"-long ⅜" lag screws and
washers

Constructing the Table

In each of 4 leg pieces, drill a
pair of pilot holes 9 inches
from bottom. Drill ½-inch
countersink holes. Mark position for pilot holes on lower leg
supports. When assembled,
supports should be flush with
edges of legs. Assemble 2 H-
shaped leg assemblies, one for
each end of table.

Nail upper leg supports
flush with top and edges of
each leg assembly, hammering
in 2 nails at each end. (Nails
should be on outer edges of
legs, leaving center clear.)

Join leg assemblies together
with 2 by 4 stretcher positioned
on edge. Prepare rails by drilling pilot and countersink holes.
Holes should be 9 inches from
each end of both 60-inch
lengths or whatever distance is
required to ensure that legs are
plumb. Insert and tighten lag
screws. Base is now complete.

Lay tabletop boards in position, spacing them equally.
Drill 2 pilot and countersink
holes at each end of every
board. Holes should be 9 inches
from ends of boards or a distance that will cause lag screws
to enter center of 2 by 4 rails.

Lower Leg Support

Upper Leg Support

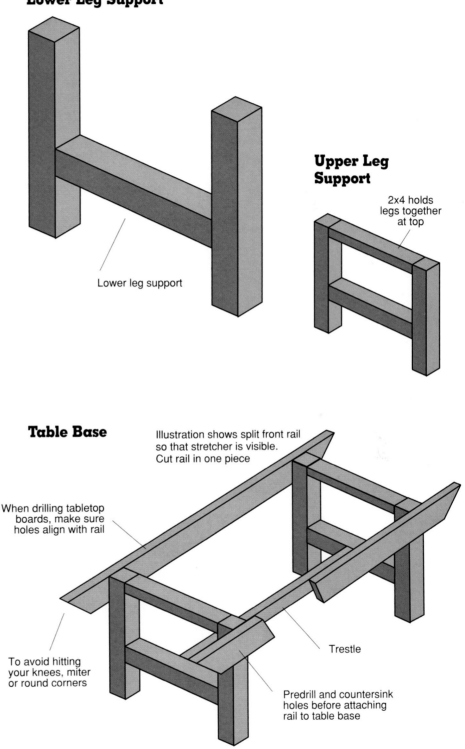

Lower leg support

2x4 holds legs together at top

Table Base

Illustration shows split front rail so that stretcher is visible. Cut rail in one piece

When drilling tabletop boards, make sure holes align with rail

To avoid hitting your knees, miter or round corners

Trestle

Predrill and countersink holes before attaching rail to table base

TRAY-TOP TABLE

Here's a versatile table that can be put to a multitude of uses when entertaining or working outside. Build it in an afternoon and use it that night.

Making the Table

This table is a piece of furniture that will become invaluable as a work counter or a serving tray. It can be carried to an outdoor dining table and act as a buffet on which to set up a salad and separate bowls of salad dressing. When it's time to serve the salad, lift the tray top off the base and carry it to the dining table. It can also be a portable bar. Set bottles, jug, and glasses on the tray. Or

flip the top over and carry it around the yard to use as a work or potting table. Draw it up beside a bed of cutting flowers and you have a stand on which to create a floral arrangement. The final result can be carried inside and the mess cleared up outside.

Finish the tray so that your table can be used as a work stand, then cleaned and used to serve food. Covering the base with tile allows for this quick change. Realize, however, that tiling the base will make it much heavier. Use thin tiles that are as light as possible. One alternative is to make the base out of laminated pieces of board lumber and paint it with several layers of marine varnish. This will provide a surface that is easy to wipe clean. Flip the tray over when you go inside. This way it will not fill with water should it rain.

In order to make this piece as versatile as possible, construct the tray top so that it merely rests on top of the base. If you are worried that guests might not realize this and might knock the tray off the base, you can screw the top permanently into position before finishing or tiling it. If you do this, it will be unnecessary to include the finger grips.

The leg attachments can be made out of square-cut pieces or, if you want a more elegant-looking table, angle-cut or shaped pieces as desired.

The tray can be made any size or shape. Just be sure that the proportions of your piece are such that they will provide good support. Directions are for making a 26½-inch-high table with a top that is approximately 25 inches square.

Materials List

26″ length 4×4 for post
4, 6″ lengths 2×2 for legs
4, 8″ lengths 2×2 for tray support
2′ square ⅝″ exterior plywood for tray base
2, 25″ lengths 1×3 for tray lip
2, 24″ lengths 1×3 for tray lip

Constructing the Table

Shape leg pieces as desired, predrill holes, and nail to leg in pinwheel fashion. (See illustration.) Be sure to create a nailing pattern that avoids hitting nails hammered in from a different direction.

Nail on tray support pieces using same pinwheel method.

Prepare 25-inch 1 by 3s for tray-top lips. (This step is unnecessary if the top will be permanent.) Drill holes in center of 1 by 3 and, using a chisel or hacksaw, join holes to make finger grips. Grips can be any size or shape that seems appropriate. Round off ends with a rasp and smooth all edges with a file and sandpaper.

Glue and screw lips to tray base. (You might want to miter corners. If you do, adjust length of lip pieces accordingly.)

Tile interior of tray or finish as desired. Or screw top to tray supports before finishing it.

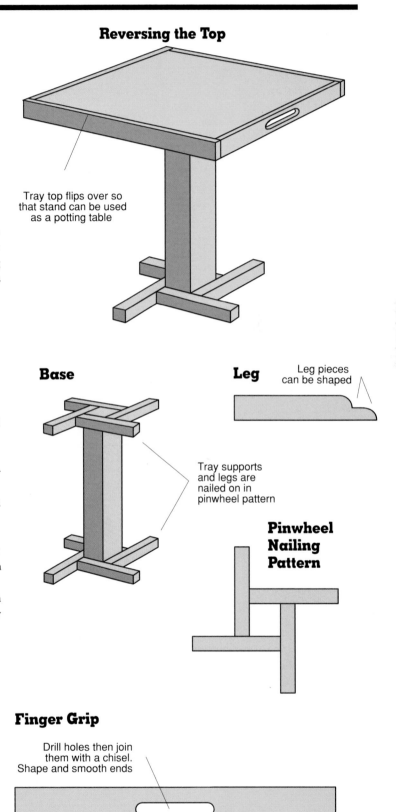

Reversing the Top

Tray top flips over so that stand can be used as a potting table

Base

Leg

Leg pieces can be shaped

Tray supports and legs are nailed on in pinwheel pattern

Pinwheel Nailing Pattern

Finger Grip

Drill holes then join them with a chisel. Shape and smooth ends

BARBECUE CART

This convenient barbecue stand can be rolled to wherever it is needed. Doors at both ends provide access to two large storage compartments that provide ample space for folding chairs, cooking utensils, charcoal, and other entertaining paraphernalia.

Making the Cart

This cart, approximately 5 feet long and 2 feet wide, is made by cladding a 2 by 4 framework with panels cut from sheets of Texture 1-11. If you use other plywood, adjust measurements accordingly. The ones given are for $^{19}/_{32}$-inch panels.

Layouts and measurements are for making a cart with two compartments. One measures approximately two feet from the door to the divider wall, the other approximately three feet. These dimensions can be altered to suit your needs. Even if you omit the divider wall, insert the nailer. It is needed to brace the top frame.

Cutting Plywood Pieces

Mark both plywood panels, following layouts shown. Use a straightedge and and a carpenter's square to accurately draw all parts on plywood. Be sure to allow for saw kerfs between sections that abut.

To get clean cuts on edges that will show, always cut plywood on the appropriate face. If hand-sawing, use a 10- to 15-point crosscut saw and place panel front face up. If using a hand-held power saw, use a plywood or combination blade and place panel front face down. If using a table saw, place panel front face up. To reduce splintering on the back side, clamp or tack scrap lumber under the cutting line.

With first cuts, reduce panel to pieces small enough for easy handling.

Panel Layout

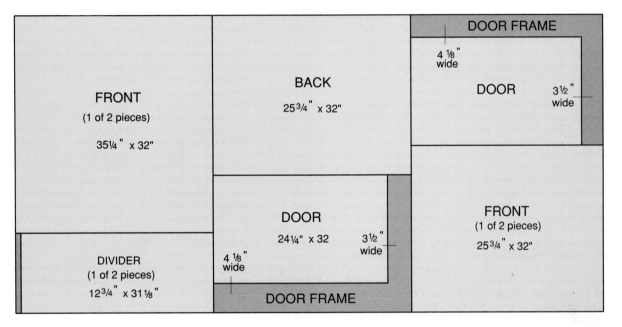

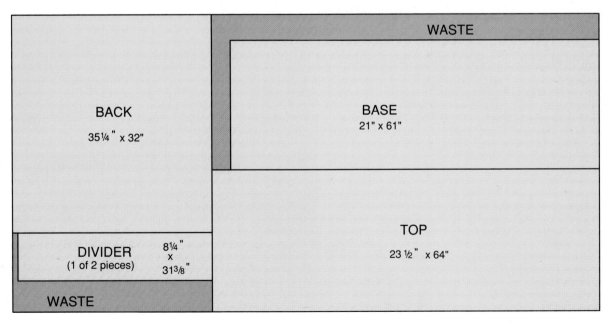

Materials List

Frame:
2, 58" lengths 2×4
2, 21" lengths 2×4
1, 18" length 2×4
6, 27¾" lengths 2×4
Cladding:
2, 4×8 panels Texture 1-11 siding
Top:
1 sheet plastic laminate 24½" × 65" or tiles for top
Trim:
2, 24½" lengths 1×2
2, 65" lengths 1×2
Hardware:
4 butt hinges
4, 3" ball casters
2 magnetic catches
2 door handles

Constructing the Cart

Start by assembling a 2 by 4 frame onto which all pieces of cut plywood are nailed.

To assemble top frame, predrill holes, then glue and nail 58-inch back and front rails between 21-inch end pieces. Within this frame, nail in divider wall pieces.

Next you need to attach 27¾- inch uprights. See illustration for position of these uprights. Along front edge, 3½-inch face is flush with and parallel to front edge. At the back, position corner posts so that 3½- inch edge face is flush with and parallel to side edge and divider wall post is flush with and parallel to back edge.

Work out how you will attach uprights without putting undue strain on first connection. (Until uprights are fastened firmly to both plywood

Exploded View

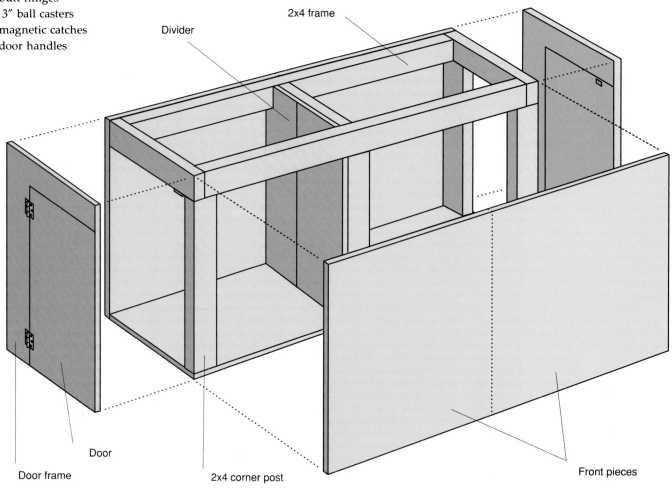

Divider

2x4 frame

Door

Door frame

2x4 corner post

Front pieces

base and top frame they will wobble.) One way is to lay base on trestles high enough to work from underneath. Stand uprights in place and lay top frame in position. Then glue and nail frame to uprights and, working from underneath, attach base to uprights. For additional strength, remember to coat both ends of uprights with glue before positioning them.

Turn framework right side up, and glue and nail plywood cladding in place in the following order. Attach divider wall pieces to front and back uprights, notching top corners as necessary. Attach both back pieces and both front pieces. Hinge doors to frames, then attach frames to ends of cart.

Attach top to cart and glue on laminate. If you prefer, tile the top or apply a surface of your choice. Trim top edge, mitering the corners.

Texture 1-11 is specifically made for outdoor use, but you will probably want to finish the wood with semitransparent or solid-color stain. If you prefer, you can paint it.

Allow stain or paint to dry before screwing on remaining hardware. Screw casters to underside of base at each corner. Attach magnetic catches at top outside corners of doors and matching positions on frame. Position handles wherever desired on front face of doors.

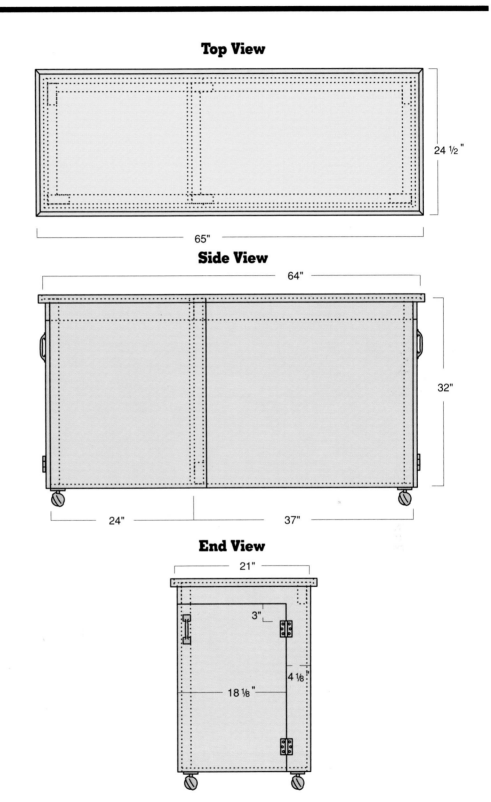

Top View

24 ½ "

65"

Side View

64"

32"

24"

37"

End View

21"

3"

4 ⅛ "

18 ⅛ "

ATTRACTING BIRDS

Observing birds provides endless pleasure. Awake before we are and active most of the day, these creatures are easy to attract if you offer them something they need and have trouble finding elsewhere. Feeders and birdhouses will ensure that your deck or patio is colorfully populated.

Plan Drawing

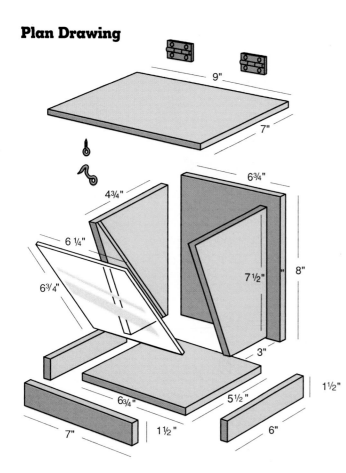

Building a Feeder

Birds eventually find feeders no matter where you put them, but you will attract a greater number and variety of birds if you place feeders in logical locations around your deck or patio. Experiment with different spots before choosing one. Once you find locations that seem to work, stick with them through the winter—birds like the location of their food sources to be predictable.

Place a feeding station in a sheltered spot within an easy flight to cover and perches. Many birds like to dart quickly to a feeder, grab a few seeds, and return to the safety of a bush or tree. Locate feeders at varying distances from the house to encourage both bold and shy birds.

If you want to only attract ground-feeding birds, a simple platform or dish will suffice. However, to interest a greater variety of birds, try a hopper-style feeder, a popular design.

Materials Required

½" exterior plywood
Piece of glass or acrylic
2 small hinges
Hook and eye
Ring-shank nails

Constructing a Hopper Feeder

Cut out pieces to dimensions indicated and treat each piece with wood preservative.

On inside faces of both side pieces, rout a slot to accept sheet of glass or acrylic.

Before nailing, drill pilot holes to prevent wood from splitting. Attach back to tray base, nailing through back piece into edge of base. Attach sides, nailing them in place through back and base pieces. Attach rails around tray base.

Set lid on top of feeder and mark screw position for hinges. Drill pilot holes and attach hinges. Also mark positions for hook and eye. (Mount hook to outside face of side piece.)

Building a Birdhouse

The way a birdhouse looks on the outside means nothing to birds. The amenities are what matter. The most critical factor is the entrance hole. If you want a house for chickadees, the diameter of the hole must be at least 1⅛ inches. If you make it 1¼ inches, the house will fill up with sparrows. Wrens, bluebirds, and several species of swallow all use houses with 1½-inch entrance holes. Anything larger will admit starlings.

Loosely mounted boxes that jiggle or sway in the wind are not attractive to birds. Screw or nail birdhouse to a post or tree.

Materials Required

½" exterior plywood
Short length ½×½ for cleats
2 small hinges
Hook and eye
Ring-shank nails

Constructing a Basic Birdhouse

Before nailing, drill pilot holes to prevent wood from splitting.

Cut out pieces to dimensions indicated and treat each piece with wood preservative before assembly.

Drill ventilation holes in top of side pieces and drainage holes in base. Using a hole-saw attachment, cut out entrance hole in front piece.

Attach cleats to inside face of front piece.

On back, front, and one side piece, measure and mark a line ½ inch from bottom. Position base so that underside matches marked line and attach.

Position second side piece and mark screw position of hinges. Drill pilot holes and attach hinges. Mark position and attach hook and eye.

Set roof in position and nail through top into back, front, and side pieces.

Plan Drawing

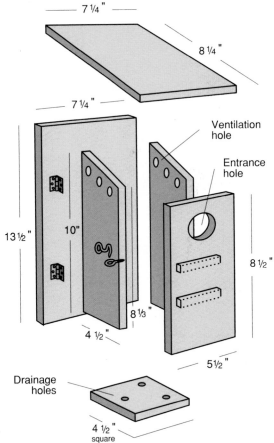

COLOR SCHEMES: CONTAINERS FOR NATURE'S DECORATIONS

As in any room, your outdoor space should be full of color and texture. Luckily you won't have to study color wheels or riffle through samples. Just call on Mother Nature to decorate your deck or patio with a profusion of leaves, flowers, trailing plants, and vines. And you never need worry about colors clashing. For some reason, in nature they all seem to work together to make a space look more inviting.

This chapter is devoted to containers in which to grow the plants that will become your decoration. On the following pages you will find an assortment of looks and sizes. Most of the featured planters are made of wood, but there are also ideas for using concrete block. Some of the projects are combined with seating.

If the sizes specified do not suit you, your space, or your plants, it is easy to alter the dimensions. However, always study the plans and the directions carefully before ordering or cutting materials.

A wall of weathered wood planks forms a neutral background for a mass of color. Potted plants are hung on this wall with the clips shown on the next page. Nail these clips to a wall and fit them around the collar of a clay pot.

Far from limiting gardening options, container gardening extends them. The major advantage is ease. You make or buy a container, fill it with soil, and plant whatever you want. There are no weeds to battle and no rows to straighten.

Container Gardening

The mobility of containers lets you color your outdoor living space almost instantly, all year round. You need never have a dull season on your deck or patio. For example, early bulbs, flowering quince, camellias, and primroses can be moved aside as petunias, alyssum, dwarf marigolds, althea, summer vegetables, and other late-spring and summer plants come into season. A few months later, these containers can take a back seat as dwarf crape myrtle and chrysanthemums come into flower and the berries of pyracantha and cleyera color brightly. The brilliant autumn foliage of dogwood, Japanese maple, and Washington thorn will dress up the outdoors well into winter, when you can depend on evergreens such as Japanese black pine, holly, and Carolina cherry laurel to provide greenery on your deck.

Setting a stage for container plants enhances the beauty of each plant, and the plant's beauty is also enhanced by the fact that it is in a container. When you put a plant in a box, tub, or pot you immediately give it a new character. It stops being a mere bush and becomes an individual shrub with its own distinction. It plays a starring role.

Plants in containers can be trained into new growth patterns. A clematis that will climb 15 feet or more can be shaped as a 3-foot-wide umbrella above a 12-inch pot. Ivy can follow a curved wire, drape with simple grace, or grow as a formal column. The geranium usually looks as though it belongs on a kitchen windowsill, but trained as a standard—a patio tree—it becomes an elegant addition to an outdoor container garden.

A shrub or small tree spotlighted by being set apart in a container is often especially striking if it is shaped or pruned into a formal topiary. The classic sweet bay and the dwarf forms of the Carolina cherry laurel can be clipped and sheared into all sorts of formal shapes. Or try your hand at bonsai, the Japanese horticultural art form.

Above: Potted plants are more effective when massed together. Here, plants are grouped in large concrete containers sunk into a gravel bed. These containers can be filled with earth or used as cachepots to conceal plastic pots. To build similar containers, look in your local building supply stores for drain or flue pipe. Or build your own forms and fill them with concrete. (See pages 17 and 31 for more on building forms.)
Right: These are the clips that are used to the potted plants shown on the previous pages.

Planter is built into the corner of a two-level deck. Because the earth is contained in a black plastic liner, it is possible to avoid a boxy structure. Seen from the upper level, the planter consists of one 2 by 8 strung between a 4 by 4 and the corner rail post. Miter-cut cap covers the two front faces. On the lower level of the deck, additional 2 by 8s are fastened along the front face of the planter.

A window box is a container that allows you to enjoy the contents from indoors as well as outside. Although there are many manufactured boxes available from garden center stores, you will probably still have to build a support. And once the support is built, it is an easy matter to make your own window box to the desired shape and size.

This planter is supported by beams that are tied into interior floor joists. Braces that support the front edge are miter-cut at both ends. At the top, they are toenailed to the beams; at the bottom, into a ledger fastened along the base of the wall.

Planting Tips

Plants growing in containers demand closer attention than the same plants growing in a flower border or a vegetable patch. When you constrict the root zone, you must compensate for the smaller area by watering and feeding more frequently. Given this fact, there are some simple tips that can help make the difference between a healthy and a sick plant and between an aggravated and a satisfied gardener.

Use a good soil mix. Good landscape soil does not necessarily make good container soil. Container growing is different from ordinary garden growing, and soil for containers must have these characteristics: fast drainage of water, plenty of air in the soil after drainage, and a reservoir of water in the soil after drainage.

Don't overfill the container. An 8-inch pot should have about 2 inches of space at the top to hold water. Doing a good job of watering is much more difficult if you fill the pot so full with soil that an adequate amount of water cannot sit before soaking through and thoroughly wetting the soil.

Use a mulch. A mulch is a protective covering spread over the top of the soil. This slows surface drying and prevents a crust from forming. Good mulches for container plants are unmilled peat moss, fir bark, small stones, and plants such as Corsican mint, Scotch or Irish moss, and chamomile.

Use double potting. By putting a pot with drainage holes inside a container with no drainage you can moderate the environment for plant roots and avoid a water-stained deck. Put a layer of gravel in the base of the exterior pot and pack the space between the two pots with perlite, unmilled sphagnum peat moss, or fir bark.

In addition to using the typical clay and plastic pots, there are many ways to display plants. Anything that holds earth can be used as a container. For example, an interesting rock has an indentation in the center that becomes home for a succulent plant (top left). A profusion of color bursts from pockets in the sides of a strawberry planter, as well as spilling over the top (top right). A barrel can be filled with earth to act as a deep planter, or used as a stand on which to display potted plants (left). A slice of tree trunk makes a natural pedestal for a potted coleus (above).

WATERING SYSTEMS

If you plan to build some of the planters shown on the following pages, you need to consider how to water the plants that will fill them. Even if you already have a watering system, the additions you are considering may necessitate extending it. Knowing how the system operates will allow you to make plans.

General Principles

In order to make intelligent choices, you need to be acquainted with the components of a watering system, how such a system works, and general installation principles. Although installation is not regulated to the same extent that electrical and garden-construction work are, it is a good idea to check local codes. Of particular importance is the connection to the supply line.

The basic installation of a manual or automatic system is as follows: The main line carries water from the meter through a backflow preventer to valves that connect with lateral lines. Each lateral line has its own valve. The main line is under constant pressure, and when the valve opens, water flows into the lateral line and out through sprinkler or emitter heads.

The number of lateral lines needed depends on the area to be covered and the type of watering required. You may need more than one line to water a lawn, but do not use one lateral line to water both lawn and shrubs. Install separate lines because lawns need water frequently for short periods; shrubs require less frequent but deeper watering.

Sprinkler heads or drip system emitters are attached to lateral lines with risers.

Watering Methods

Plants can be watered with a hand-held hose, by a sprinkler system, by a drip system, or by any combination of these methods.

Both sprinkler systems and drip systems can be manually or automatically operated. The only difference is the type of valve used. A manual watering system is equipped with manually operated valves, meaning you must be there to turn valves on and off. Manual valves cost less than automatic valves. There is no need for a controller, but the remainder of the system—pipe, sprinkler heads, and other components—will cost the same as for an automatic system.

Automatic valves, also called remote control valves (RCVs), are electrically or, sometimes, hydraulically operated. Valves are activated by a controller, which can be preset to water any part of the garden for any amount of time on any day of the week and at any hour of day. This means that watering can be accomplished during the early morning hours—from 3 to 7 a.m. when the yard is not in use, when general water usage is lowest and therefore water pressure highest, and when the wind is usually lightest. Watering plants early in the morning allows them to dry out during the sunny part of the day. This prevents mildew and fungus from forming.

Hand Watering

There is little to say about hand watering. Obviously it is not as expensive as installing an irrigation system, but it is time-consuming and less efficient, and you have to be there to do the watering.

Sprinkler Systems

Sometimes referred to as overhead irrigation, this system consists of pipe, valves, and heads that spray water in different patterns over planted areas. However, a sprinkler system provides only surface watering—not particularly helpful to deep-rooted trees and shrubs.

Drip Systems

A drip irrigation system is most useful for slow, deep watering of individual trees, shrubs, and planters. It should not be considered for watering lawns or large bedding areas.

Because it operates under low pressure (5 to 25 pounds per square inch), the materials are inexpensive. But this savings is offset by the fact that water must be carried to each plant, which requires a lot of material.

Instead of sprinkler heads, a drip system uses small emitters plugged into the end of tubing. These emitters dribble water into the soil at the rate of a few gallons per hour, providing slow, thorough, and deep watering. Very little water is lost due to runoff or evaporation.

Components

There is a tremendous variety of watering system equipment available in many styles, sizes, and materials. Quality and price vary considerably, and equipment is sold for residential, commercial, and industrial situations. Choose good-quality equipment suitable for residential use.

You can obtain catalogs and equipment from irrigation equipment manufacturers or supply houses. Check your local telephone directory for listings. Most home center stores and some garden centers offer these products as well.

The most commonly used components of a residential watering system are briefly described below.

Pipe

Nowadays, PVC (polyvinyl chloride) pipe is almost always used. It has all but replaced galvanized steel because it is easier to handle, is fast to assemble, and will not corrode. Whereas galvanized pipe requires difficult cutting and threading, PVC can be fused (glued) together using a special solvent.

PVC is manufactured under two rating systems: schedule rating and class rating. Schedule-rated pipe has walls of uniform thickness regardless of pipe diameter. The walls of class-rated pipe vary in thickness—the greater the diameter, the thicker the wall—thus the pressure rating remains the same regardless of the diameter of the pipe. Class 200, for example, will carry 200 psi (pounds per square inch) of pressure before bursting. Schedule-rated pipe is stronger in the smaller diameters and thus is most often specified for fittings and risers. Class-rated pipe is stronger and more dependable in larger diameters and therefore is often used for main lines.

Residential systems are generally composed of pipe in classes 315, 200, and 160, and in schedule 40 for fittings and some main lines. Lateral lines are generally class 200 or the less expensive class 160. The class or schedule, the manufacturer, and the NSF stamp showing that it meets the requirements of the National Sanitary Foundation are all stamped on the pipe.

PVC pipe will deteriorate and weaken if exposed to sunlight for any length of time. To prevent this, store all pipe in a shaded area and bury it completely after installing it.

Fittings

Fittings join pipe sections and connect the sprinkler heads to the lateral line piping. They come in a variety of sizes and shapes: tees, elbows, sleeves, risers, nipples, and unions.

PVC elbows and sleeves are usually slip-fitted, meaning that pipe slips into the fitting and is glued in place. Other fittings, such as unions, risers, and sometimes nipples, are threaded on one or both ends and screw onto the pipe. Some fittings are labeled. For example, SST indicates that two openings are the slip type and one opening is threaded; SSS indicates that all three openings are slip-jointed.

Schedule 40 PVC is normally used for fittings. Where strength is important, such as in risers, schedule 80 might be more appropriate.

Valves

There are two types of valves: manual and automatic. Both operate like any faucet: No water passes through the valve until it is opened.

Manual Valves

A manual valve is usually placed in a box just below ground level. It is operated either by a faucet or with a valve key (a long rod with a fork on one end).

Automatic Valves

Automatic valves have solenoids attached to them. The solenoid is connected to the controller by two low-voltage wires. When the setting on the controller indicates that watering should begin, an electrical current is sent through the wires and the valve opens. When the watering cycle is complete, the current is shut off and the valve closes. Control wires are usually buried in the same trench as the pipe.

Some automatic valves are hydraulic, connected to the controller with small-diameter, flexible tubing. Water in the tubing is pressurized. The valve opens when pressure is released and closes when pressure is applied, or vice versa. Because of freezing problems with a hydraulic system, electrically operated valves are much more popular.

Controllers

Controllers, sometimes called clocks, turn the water on and off automatically. Today, state-of-the-art controllers can be programmed to turn on water at any hour, on any day, and for any period of time. Repeat cycles allow you to water certain areas more than once a day. Digital readouts advise you of the options and how to program them. Less expensive models and models with fewer options are also available.

Controllers come in a variety of sizes and capacities. Capacity is determined by the number of stations a controller can handle. Typically, one station operates one valve; thus, a six-station controller can operate six automatic valves.

Heads

There are hundreds of sprinkler heads on the market. They are offered in many shapes, materials, sizes, and patterns, and with a variety of internal components and operational requirements involving pressure and flow rate. Looking through irrigation catalogs is the best way to select the proper heads for your system.

Types of Heads

Impact or pop-up heads are designed for lawns and ground cover. These lie flush with the ground surface, making them less visible and facilitating mowing. They pop up when water is discharged and are designed to distribute water over a relatively flat area.

For larger lawns, gear-driven heads can be used. These are larger heads contained in a plastic or steel housing. The nozzle is directed back and forth by a system of gears.

Shrub heads (also suitable for beds) distribute water in confined areas and are sold in a variety of spray patterns. Bubbler heads are set close to the ground and bubble water rather than spray it.

Pattern

The spray pattern may cover a full circle or a half, third, or quarter circle. The height of the arc determines the diameter of the area sprayed.

Coverage

Coverage concerns the distance water is thrown from the head. This can be as little as 3 feet or as much as 150 feet. Heads can usually be adjusted to allow for a range of coverage.

Drip irrigation systems are a time-saving convenience. Once installed they require little attention and save water by reducing evaporation loss. There are many types of emitter heads that fit into flexible tubing.

Materials

Heads are generally made out of PVC, brass, and steel. Plastic is the least expensive and possibly the most suitable material because it is easy to maintain. Brass was once the primary material for sprinkler heads, but its use is diminishing due to cost and maintenance problems. The large heads used in parks and on golf courses to cover thousands of square feet of surface area are made of steel or a combination of steel and plastic, and are expensive. The internal components—gears, couplings, springs, and nozzles—can be made of any of these materials.

Emitters

Emitters are the heads that supply water in drip irrigation systems. They are generally made of plastic, come in a variety of styles, and fit into a flexible ½- or ¾-inch-diameter hose.

Some emitters are connected to lengths of ⅛-inch tubing so that they can be moved around.

Gate Valves

A gate valve is a manually operated valve installed on the main line between the meter and backflow preventer so that the entire system can be shut down in case of emergency or for repairs. It is called a gate valve because of the way it operates: When the handle is turned, a gate within the valve rises to allow water to pass through.

Gate valves are convenient but not essential components; many systems are installed with no such device. Other systems have several valves at critical points.

Quick-Coupling Valves

Known as a QCV, or quick coupler, this type of valve is much like a hose bibb. (See page 95.) It is installed on a main (pressurized) line so that the top is flush with the grade. A flip cap permits insertion of a coupler that, when turned, opens the valve. A hose or sprinkler head is attached to the coupler.

QCVs can be distributed around the system. They are generally placed in areas where you might want to plug in a hose for hand watering.

You could build an inexpensive system using QCVs and sprinkler heads that plug in when needed instead of being permanently installed.

Check Valves

A check valve is a small device installed at the base of a sprinkler head or within a run of pipe that allows water to flow in one direction only.

Check valves are used on sloped lines to prevent water in the system from continuing to flow out of heads when the automatic valve is closed.

Drain Valves

Drain valves come in various sizes and types and are primarily used on systems that must be drained in winter to prevent water from freezing in the pipes.

These valves are set at the lowest point in the system and are opened to drain out all residual water.

Hose Bibbs

A hose bibb is a faucet generally mounted on the exterior of the house or to a standpipe. The threaded lip allows you to attach a hose. Regardless of whether or not you install a watering system, you need hose bibbs close to any area in which you use water.

Meters

The water meter is installed on your property between the house and municipal supply line to measure the amount of water used both inside and outside the house. Chances are a meter will already be in place. Check with the local utility company, which usually installs them, if you cannot locate a meter near your home.

Backflow Preventers

A backflow preventer is a device installed in the service line leading from the municipal supply main to the house. It is located on the house side of the meter, downstream from the connection to the potable water supply. The purpose of this device is to prevent any water that has flowed back into the watering system from reaching the city water supply or mixing with the potable water supply to the house.

Virtually every community insists that a backflow preventer be installed as a part of a watering system. This requirement is to prevent contaminants from reaching general water supplies and should always be met.

The most common backflow preventers are antisiphon valves, vacuum breakers, and atmospheric breakers. These are simple, inexpensive devices that operate by allowing air to enter the highest point of the system and break any vacuum that might siphon water back into the main supply. More sophisticated preventers, involving check valves and pressure operation, are usually only demanded on larger commercial systems. Be sure to check local codes for requirements.

Terminology

As well as the equipment involved in a watering system, there are some common terms you should understand when designing a watering system and choosing equipment.

Flow Rate

The flow rate is a measurement of water pressure expressed in gallons per minute (gpm)—how many gallons pass through a meter, pipe, or head every minute. Every sprinkler head requires a minimum amount of water pressure in order to operate properly. Design your system so that the last head (the one farthest from the valve) receives at least the minimum gpm needed.

Frequency and Period

Frequency indicates how often a given area is watered. Period refers to the length of time the water is on. Many combinations of frequency and period of watering can be programmed into a controller.

Main Line

The main line carries the supply of water under pressure from the meter through the backflow preventer to valves where it is distributed to lateral lines and then to the heads. The main line is the largest line in the system. There may be only one main line or several, depending on the extent of your irrigation system.

Lateral Lines

Lateral lines receive water from the main line when the valve is open. Each lateral line, which is generally smaller than the main line, must have a valve.

Pressure

Pressure measures the force exerted against the walls of a pipe or a head and is expressed in pounds per square inch (psi). You must know the pressure and flow rate of your system in order to select suitable sprinkler heads. Typically, a head is designated as operating with 20 gpm at 40 psi. As pressure is reduced, the amount of flow is usually reduced.

Relative Costs of Watering Systems

The cost of installion depends on the extent and sophistication of the watering system.

The least expensive way to water lawns and plants is by hand. This requires plenty of hose bibbs as well as plenty of hoses so that you can reach all the areas of your yard.

The quick-coupler system is the least expensive requiring a water-meter connection, a backflow preventer and manual shutoff valve, a main line, quick-coupling valves, and a supply of plug-in quick couplers that you move from place to place. Although this is a manual system, the lines are permanent and it can be upgraded to an automatic system at a later date.

Automatic systems are more expensive to install than manual ones, and the larger the system, the higher the cost. Each sprinkler head and each control valve adds to the cost.

Drip systems can save you money due to lower water consumption, and the cost of installation is no higher than for conventional watering systems. The advantage is that water enters the soil slowly and naturally, thereby minimizing runoff, evaporation, and costly erosion problems.

CANTILEVERED PLANTER BENCH

This planter and bench combination is designed to be secured to 4 by 4 posts. One of these could be an existing structural post.

Building the Planter Bench

This planter requires 45-degree bevel cuts (miters) on edges of planter walls, facing strips, nailer, and 2 by 4s in the corner section of the bench.

Materials List

3 or 4, 4×4 posts
12, 21" lengths 2×6 for planter walls
8, 22" lengths ½×1 for trim
4, 42" lengths 2×4 for frame
2, 39" lengths 2×4 for dividers
8, 15" lengths 2×2 for spacers
1, 19½" length 2×2 for nailer
8, 24" lengths 2×4 for rectangular bench sections
4, 13½" lengths 2×4 for corner bench section

Constructing the Planter Bench

Set 4 posts so that they measure 18 inches apart from outside faces and 16½ inches above decking level. Miter-cut edges of 2 by 6s so that they measure 21 inches on outside face. Each of the 4 planter walls is built by nailing three 2 by 6s to posts. Apply glue at ends before nailing in place.

Miter-cut edges of 2 by 4 frame pieces so that they measure 42 inches on outside face.

Cut 1½-inch-wide notches, 3 inches deep, 15 inches from end of 39-inch-long dividers. Notch pieces together and tack them to frame temporarily. Place frame over planter and check for fit. When satisfied, remove frame and disassemble dividers. Apply glue in notch

and to ends of dividers. Drill countersinks and screw permanently to frame.

Glue and nail 2 by 2 spacers within frame. Position them as shown in illustration, flush with bottom edge of frame and level with each other.

In order to provide a nailer for miter-cut bench planks, you must install a diagonal nailer. (See illustration.) Measure distance between inside corners—it should be approximately 19½ inches. Make a mark at center point on one face of nailer and miter-cut corners on both sides of this mark. Do the same at other end. Glue and nail this nailer so that it is flush with bottom edge of frame and top edge of 2 by 2 spacers.

Place frame over planter so that top of frame is 16½ inches from ground and flush with top of posts. Check for level, then screw through dividers into posts and along both inside planter walls. Also screw through frame into both outside planter walls. Countersink heads and fill all holes.

Lay bench planks in rectangular sections.

Set corner bench planks across end, spacing them to match other bench planks. Lay a straightedge so that it intersects corner of frame and corner of divider. Mark the diagonal line across all 4 planks. Remove planks and cut each one to length. The waste pieces, turned upside down and placed in reverse order, will complete miter-cut corner section. Lay all pieces in place and check for fit. If you need to make adjustments, do so on square-cut ends. When satisfied, nail planks to spacers and to diagonal nailer.

Top View

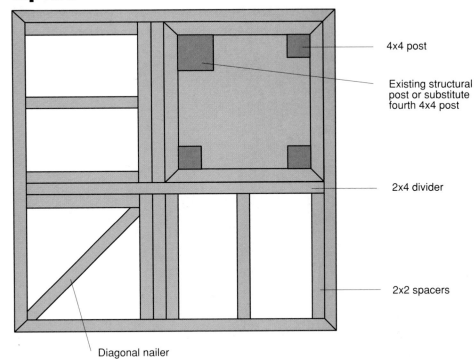

4x4 post

Existing structural post or substitute fourth 4x4 post

2x4 divider

2x2 spacers

Diagonal nailer

Side View

2x4 frame around cantilevered bench section

Trim covers gaps between 2x6 boards

Notching Dividers

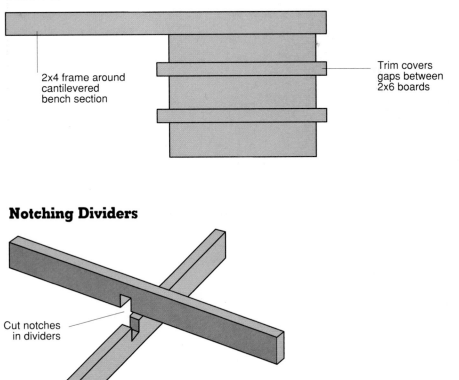

Cut notches in dividers

Tending planters can be backbreaking work. This combination planter and bench unit offers a place to rest your tools when you are working on the plants or rest yourself when you are sitting and enjoying them.

Building Planter Seating Units

These planters, which act as supports for slatted benches, are composed of five easy-to-build frames stacked on top of each other. Both planters and benches are constructed of 2 by 4s on edge. Use a naturally durable wood such as Western red cedar to make a handsome and sturdy seating unit.

The illustrations show planters that are approximately 24 inches square and 18 inches high supporting benches that are 8 feet long by approximately 12 inches wide. It is simple to alter these dimensions as well as the configuration. You may prefer just two planters supporting one bench, or you can add extra benches and planters and form a star shape in the middle of a patio.

Materials List

For each planter:
20, 22½" lengths 2×4 for sides
4, 16" lengths 2×2 for nailing posts
6, 22" lengths 1×4s for base
For each bench:
7, 8' lengths 2×4

Constructing Planter Seating Units

To make planters, predrill and nail four 22½-inch 2 by 4s into a frame. Lap pieces alternately as shown. Make 5 frames for each planter section.

Attach base to one frame. Lay equally spaced 1 by 4s across. Predrill and nail to frame. If you feel gaps between boards are insufficient drainage, drill ¾-inch holes.

Stack 2 frames on top of base frame, alternating corner joints. Fit nailing posts snuggly in each corner and nail through posts into sides. Last 2 frames will be attached after making bench. Complete 3 layers of total number of planters to be made and set aside.

To make bench, cut 2 by 4s to length required, realizing that approximately 3½ inches will be under top layers of planters. Laminate boards into a solid block by gluing face surfaces. Clamp with pipe clamps until glue is completely dry, or drill boards and join with threaded rod as described for bench shown on page 73.

When bench is complete, measure width and cut opening in fourth frame to accept this width.

Set up partially assembled planters in their final positions (it will be very difficult to move this unit once it is complete). Set benches on top of third frame and lock them into position with cutouts in fourth frame. Set final frame in position. Nail through nailing posts into fourth and fifth frames.

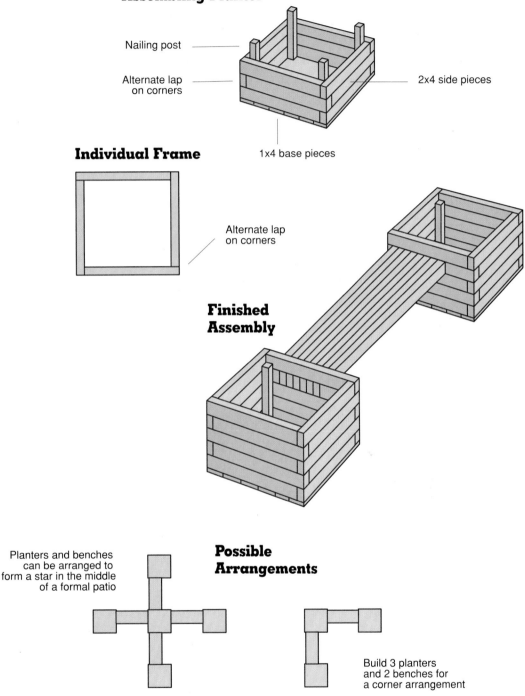

Assembling Planter

Nailing post

Alternate lap on corners

2x4 side pieces

1x4 base pieces

Individual Frame

Alternate lap on corners

Finished Assembly

Possible Arrangements

Planters and benches can be arranged to form a star in the middle of a formal patio

Build 3 planters and 2 benches for a corner arrangement

LEGGED PLANTER

As long as you own a saw and a hammer, there is nothing to stop you from building several of these planters in an afternoon. You can even have the lumberyard cut lengths of redwood for you to make the job simpler.

Building the Legged Planter

As with all the projects in this book, the dimensions given are based on a 2 by 4 measuring exactly 1½ inches by 3½ inches. If your lumber varies, lay out each planter wall, measure it, and cut nailers to that measurement minus 3 inches.

Dimensions allow for a three-inch leg. Change the length of the corner pieces if you prefer the look of a more exaggerated leg.

Materials List

18, 14" lengths 2×4 for sides
8, 17" lengths 2×4 for legs
2, 21½" lengths 2×4 for nailers
2, 18" lengths 2×4 for nailers
21" square ⅝" exterior plywood for base

Constructing the Legged Planter

Spread glue along edges of five 14-inch lengths and lay them out so that pieces butt tightly together and are flush top and bottom. Lay a 17-inch length at both ends so that top is flush and bottom extends 3 inches to form leg. Center a 21½-inch length across these boards, flush with bottom of shorter pieces. Nail it in place. Repeat procedure for opposing wall.

Spread glue along edges of four 14-inch lengths with a 17-inch length at both ends and lay them out, positioning them as before. Center 18-inch nailer across these boards and fasten as before. Repeat procedure for opposing wall.

You now have 2 walls (front and back) composed of 7 boards and 2 (sides) of 6 boards. Stand these up and nail them together at corners.

Drill drainage holes in plywood base and drop it in place on top of nailers.

Exploded View

17" length

14" length

Nailer

MITERED PLANTER

A basic box is made more attractive by adding a design of grooves cut with a saw or a router. The corners are mitered so that the design flows around all four sides.

Building the Planter

Building this planter is merely a matter of joining the four sides and adding a base. The size of the box will depend on the look you desire, the type of plants you plan to grow in it, and the size of the lumber you plan to use.

Because of the tailored look, it is recommended that you use a single piece of board lumber to form each side. This means the board will have to be wide enough to provide the desired depth of the planter. An alternative is to laminate two pieces of board together and incorporate the seam into the grooved design, routing it in the same manner as the other lines. Directions are to make a planter that is 18 inches square and approximately 11 inches deep.

The design is composed of grooves cut into the face of the boards. These grooves can be as wide and as deep as you like and can be made with one or more passes of a saw blade or by using a router. Grooves between 3/8 inch and 1/2 inch deep and wide would be appropriate. In keeping with current fashion, the design shown is simple and geometric. However, depending on your skill and your tools, you can create any pattern that appeals to you. If you want to get more

ambitious, inlay the grooves or use them for banding straps.

To prevent rotting, treat the interior of the planter with a preservative and line with polyethylene.

Materials List

1, 8' length 2×12 for sides
2, 16½" lengths 2×4 for base support
15" square ¾" exterior plywood for base

Constructing the Planter

Grooved design should be applied before cutting board into pieces. This way, you are assured of a perfect match. It can be done after sides are cut, in which case you must mark carefully to make sure design will flow around corners.

Miter-cut 2 by 12 into 4 pieces all 18 inches long. To prevent mitered corners from opening up, join sides with screws. Predrill screw holes, making sure design matches and edges of boards are flush. Glue and screw sides together.

Out of 2 by 4, cut 2 pieces 16½ inches or to a length equal to outer dimension of planter minus 1½ inches. Center and nail 2 by 4s on the bottom.

Drill drainage holes in plywood base and drop it in place. Line planter with polyethylene, stapling it to sides and piercing it to provide drainage.

Mitered Sides

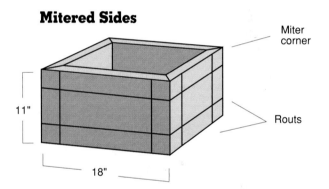

Miter corner

11"

Routs

18"

Base Supports

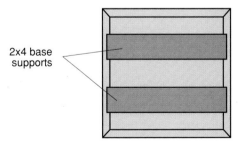

2x4 base supports

HORIZONTALLY PLANKED PLANTER

This tailored-looking planter has double-walled sides and a wide cap to give it a substantial appearance.

Building the Planter

To make sure that your planter will stay looking as good as new, use construction heart redwood to build sections that will come in contact with soil.

Materials List

Construction Heart:
4, 15" lengths 4×4 for corner posts
16, 22½" lengths 1×4 for interior walls
4, 22½" lengths 2×6 for base
2, 24½" lengths 2×4 for legs
Construction Common:
16, 22½" lengths 1×4 for outer walls
4, 26½" lengths 1×4 for cap
8, 15" lengths 2×2 for nailing posts

Constructing the Planter

Attach 2 by 2 nailing posts to 4 by 4 corner posts, using 12d nails. Center 2 by 2s so that 1 by 4 sides will fit flush with outer faces of 4 by 4 posts.

Using construction heart material for the face that will come in contact with earth, complete 2 walls, both inside and out, to form an L-shaped section as shown; space 1 by 4s evenly along post. First and last boards should be flush with top and bottom of post. Nail to posts with two 6d nails at both ends. Construct last 2 walls in the same manner.

On underside of planter position 2 by 4s as shown. Recess them approximately 2 inches and attach to nailing posts with two 12d nails at each end. Turn planter right side up.

Drill two 1-inch drainage holes in 2 of the 2 by 6 base pieces. Lay all 4 base pieces in bottom of planter.

For the top cap, attach 1 by 4s flush with outer wall. Use two 6d nails at each board end, penetrating 4 by 4 at one end and 2 by 2 at other. For a more finished appearance, countersink nails and fill with nonoily wood filler.

Line interior with polyethylene. Pierce holes in base in order to provide drainage.

Exploded View

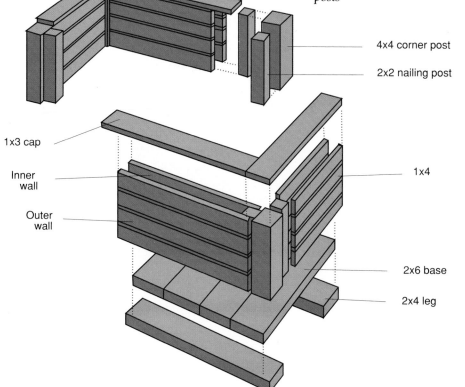

4x4 corner post

2x2 nailing post

1x3 cap

Inner wall

Outer wall

1x4

2x6 base

2x4 leg

PLANT PEDESTAL

If you can stack wood, you can make this pedestal and then top it off with a favorite potted plant or a piece of garden sculpture.

Making a Pedestal

Making this pedestal is as simple as it looks. It is composed of lengths of 4 by 4 that are stacked in pairs until the tower is the height you wish.

In order to keep this pedestal from appearing too utilitarian, it is a good idea to treat or paint the wood so that it looks special. To paint the wood, first prime it; then spray paint to get a smooth finish.

Bleach is a popular finish for wood used indoors and also blends in well outside. See page 10 for more information on bleaching wood.

Neither glue nor nails are necessary; the weight of the lumber will hold this structure in place. It is more fun to be able to disassemble the pedestal and move it or make two smaller ones topped with trays to use as tables.

Unless you want the pedestal to look more like a wood pile than a sculpture, it is important to lay pieces exactly. 4 by 4 pairs should be parallel to each other and perpendicular to pairs above and below.

If you are building a table-height stack, all ends should be flush and all overhangs an identical distance. However, the designer of this pedestal points out that if you build a high stack, it will look better and more anchored to the ground if the overhang on each alternate layer increases very slightly. For example, the second pair might be positioned 6 inches from ends of the first pair; the fourth pair, 6½ inches; the sixth pair, 7 inches; and so on. As there is no nailing or gluing involved, experiment with the amount of overhang until you get a stack with proportions that please you.

The finished pedestal will be impossible to move intact. It should be stacked in the location where it will be used.

Materials Required

4×4 cut into required lengths
Paint, stain, or bleach (optional)

Constructing a Pedestal

Lay first pair of 4 by 4s on a flat surface, making sure they are perfectly parallel to each other. Lay second pair exactly perpendicular to the first pair. Decide on amount of overlap desired and measure this distance. Lay third pair so that ends are exactly flush with first pair. Lay fourth pair either flush with second pair or ½ inch further in. (See explanation above.) Continue in this manner until you reach the desired height.

The final layer acts as a shelf for your plant or sculpture. Use as many evenly spaced pieces as appropriate or top tower with a slab of slate or marble.

# ERB GARDEN

Stack individual frames into a garden of any
shape or size. If you position the arrangement
close to the kitchen door, you will be able to
cook with fresh herbs and look out on a
fragrant garden.

Building the Planters

Although this herb garden looks complicated, it is amazingly simple to build. The garden is composed of simple frames with lapped corners that are built on a module. The outside dimensions of a square frame are 15 by 15 by 6 inches deep; a rectangular frame, 15 by 30 inches, also 6 inches deep. These frames can then be stacked at will to create an interestingly shaped garden made of planter boxes of different depths.

If this garden is positioned close to a water source, a sprinkler or drip system can be installed. (See pages 92 to 95.) Thin hose can be concealed between the frames.

Frames used at the bottom of the tower will need bases. Make these bases by nailing on pieces of exterior plywood. As you get higher up the tower, there will be occasions when you will want to cantilever a frame that will also need a base. These bases can also be nailed on the underside or, if you want to conceal them, supported by cleats nailed to inside of frame. If you don't want to go to this trouble, you can merely line the planter with polyethylene as long as there is earth in a lower planting area to support the liner.

You can keep on adding to this garden, and it is not necessary to plant all areas. You could top a stack of square frames with a baking dish filled with water. Birds bathing in the water will splash the nearby plants. You could fill a cantilevered frame with special stones or beach finds. One frame could be filled with sand and contain a desert garden.

Materials Required

2×6 board lumber for sides
Exterior plywood for bases
2×4 board lumber for legs
2×2 for support cleats

Building the Planters

Cut 2 by 6 into as many 15-inch and 30-inch pieces as required. Paint or dip pieces in preservative before assembling. Predrill ends and nail pieces together to make individual frames.

On frames that will act as base of garden, nail 13½-inch square of plywood to square frame, 13½-inch by 28½-inch piece of plywood to rectangular one. Drill holes in plywood base to provide drainage. Stack individual frames on top of each other, alternating joint pattern and twisting and cantilevering frames to suit.

On cantilevered frames, nail 2 by 2 cleats cut to a length equivalent to cantilever. Cut an appropriate-sized piece of plywood, drill drainage holes, and drop base into position.

Rectangular Frame

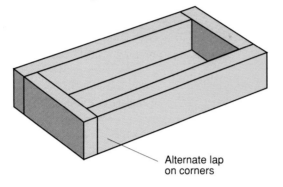

Alternate lap on corners

Bottom View

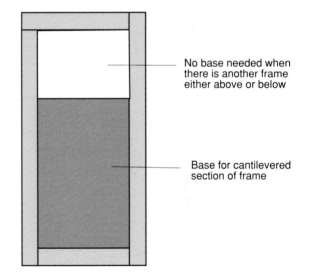

No base needed when there is another frame either above or below

Base for cantilevered section of frame

FLOWERING TREE

It's as easy to make this tree flower as it is to build it. Merely position the tree in the sunshine and top each shelf with a colorful potted plant.

Building the Tree

It is easy to build this tree even if your carpentry skills are very limited. Facenail the shelf supports and top them with square or rectangular shelves. However, if you pride yourself as a craftsperson, you will probably want to notch the post, inset the supports, and shape the shelves in one of the ways illustrated or cut a shape of your own design.

This project is shown as a tree that can be moved around. However, you could also use this idea to decorate an uninteresting structural support.

If the posts that support an overhead structure look too utilitarian, attach shelf supports and ring the post with potted plants. (Do not cut notches into a structural post—doing so will weaken it.) The post on the unattached end of a fence or screen is another candidate for plant shelves. If you nail supports to more than one post, you can attach a shelf that extends across a section of the fence. Be sure that the board you use as a shelf is strong enough to span the distance and not sag under the weight of potted plants.

If you are concerned that pots may blow off or get knocked off, cut holes in the shelves. Realize, however, that this means the base of the pot will hang below the shelf and you may want to allow more space between shelves.

Because none of the dimensions is critical, this is a perfect project to use up scrap lumber. Make the tree to any height that suits and with as many shelves as you wish.

Materials Required

1 straight 4 by 4 or 6 by 6 post of the height required
$1\times$ or $2\times$ material for 4 leg supports (if required)
1×2 for shelf supports
Exterior plywood or scrap lumber for shelves

Constructing the Tree

Place post across sawhorses or on a workbench and chamfer top end, working with a rasp, plane, or saw.

Cut leg pieces to length suitable to provide a sturdy base for the tree. Shape leg pieces as desired and nail to bottom of post in pinwheel pattern. (See page 79.)

Mark positions of shelf supports and, if you plan to inset them, notch post accordingly. Position shelf supports, making sure they are level and flush with one another, then either facenail or inset them. Attach with glue and nails.

Cut and shape shelves to suit and, if required, cut holes large enough for pot to drop in a couple of inches.

Possible Shelf Shapes

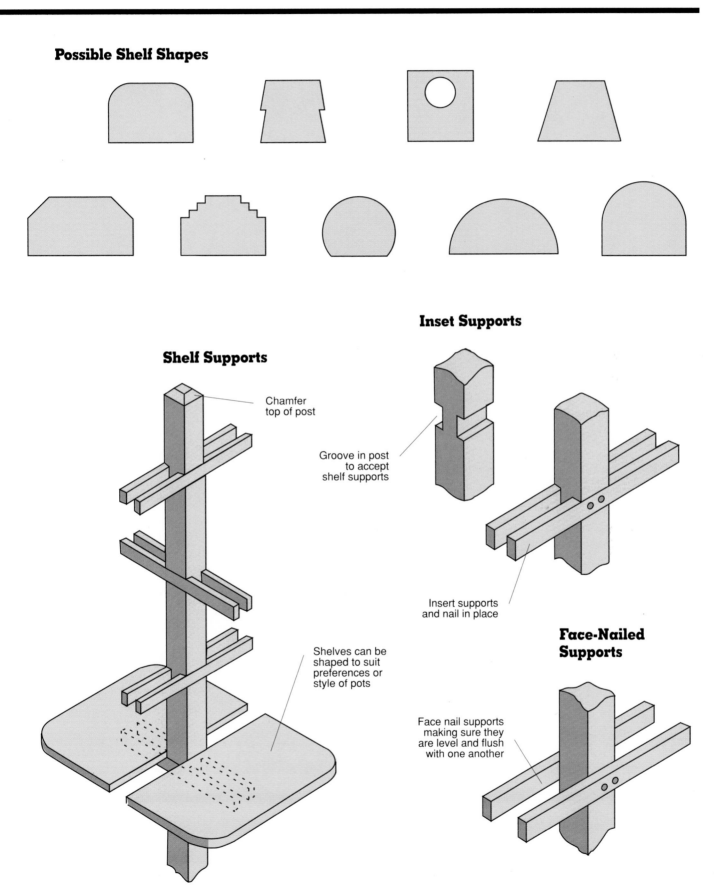

Shelf Supports

Chamfer top of post

Shelves can be shaped to suit preferences or style of pots

Inset Supports

Groove in post to accept shelf supports

Insert supports and nail in place

Face-Nailed Supports

Face nail supports making sure they are level and flush with one another

FLOWERING WALL

Stack concrete blocks to make a wall or arrange them to form an interesting flowering sculpture. Build walls with cells all facing in one direction or rotate blocks so that the wall will bloom on all sides.

Building a Wall

Planters can be made out of materials other than wood. One alternative is concrete block, which withstands both natural weathering and moisture due to watering.

Types of Blocks

Concrete block is divided into two main categories: building blocks and decorative blocks. Both types are readily available at any building supply store. Concrete building block has become a generic term for blocks made of many different materials. These include cement, cinder, and even shale, clay, or pumice. Cinder blocks are heavy, weighing around 50 pounds per block, while clay or pumice blocks weigh about 30 pounds each, and concrete blocks around 40 pounds. Bear this in mind if you will be positioning your flower wall on a deck.

Standard building blocks are nominally 8 inches wide, 8 inches high, and 16 inches long. All dimensions are actually 3/8 inch less to allow for the mortar joint. In addition, blocks are sold in 4-, 6-, 10-, and 12-inch widths. There are also 8-inch square blocks, called half blocks.

Decorative blocks are available in a variety of patterns and materials, a few of which are shown. They are generally 8 inches square and 4 inches wide. Intersperse them in a large wall for visual relief.

Mortar for concrete block is similar to that used for brick, but it should be a little stiffer to bear the additional weight. Use any mortar mix but add a little less water. Mix no more than you can use in about one hour. Unlike brick, concrete block should not be wetted before mortar is applied.

Planting the Wall

Not all the holes have to be planted. If you use trailing plants, realize that foliage will cover a large area. The wall can be made more interesting by including some of the decorative blocks that are also available at the builder's yard. This is a project for a creator, and anything goes.

The method of planting your wall or sculpture will depend on the direction of the holes in your finished arrangement. In some cases you can merely wedge in a plastic pot. If holes point in directions that make this infeasible, remove the plant from its container and wrap it in moss or polyethylene before poking it into a hole. (If you use polyethylene, pierce it in several places to provide drainage.)

Materials Required

Concrete blocks
Mortar mix

Constructing the Wall

Before mixing the mortar, do as many dry layouts as necessary until you find a form that pleases you. Make a plan of this shape so that when you dismantle it, you will remember how to put it back together in the same way.

Realize that it is necessary to build the sculpture in position. Once built, you will not be able to move it without cracking mortar joints. If you are building on a wood deck or other finished surface, protect the surrounding area.

Spread mortar onto all faces that will be in contact with the next block to be laid, press in place, and trowel off excess.

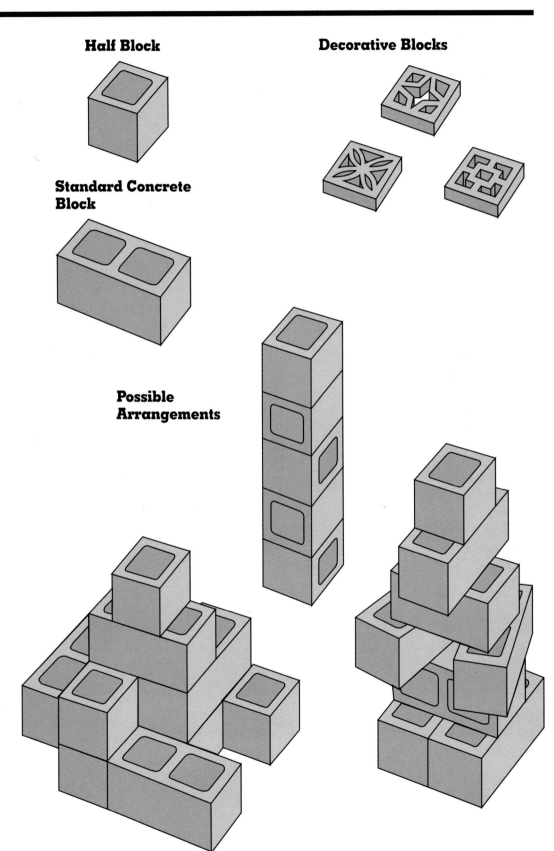

Half Block

Standard Concrete Block

Decorative Blocks

Possible Arrangements

U.S./Metric Measure Conversion Chart

	Symbol	When you know:	Multiply by:	To find:	Rounded Measures for Quick Reference		
		Formulas for Exact Measures					
Mass (Weight)	oz	ounces	28.35	grams	1 oz		= 30 g
	lb	pounds	0.45	kilograms	4 oz		= 115 g
	g	grams	0.035	ounces	8 oz		= 225 g
	kg	kilograms	2.2	pounds	16 oz	= 1 lb	= 450 g
					32 oz	= 2 lb	= 900 g
					36 oz	= 2¼ lb	= 1000 g (1 kg)
Volume	tsp	teaspoons	5.0	milliliters	¼ tsp	= 1/24 oz	= 1 ml
	tbsp	tablespoons	15.0	milliliters	½ tsp	= 1/12 oz	= 2 ml
	fl oz	fluid ounces	29.57	milliliters	1 tsp	= 1/6 oz	= 5 ml
	c	cups	0.24	liters	1 tbsp	= ½ oz	= 15 ml
	pt	pints	0.47	liters	1 c	= 8 oz	= 250 ml
	qt	quarts	0.95	liters	2 c (1 pt)	= 16 oz	= 500 ml
	gal	gallons	3.785	liters	4 c (1 qt)	= 32 oz	= 1 liter
	ml	milliliters	0.034	fluid ounces	4 qt (1 gal)	= 128 oz	= 3¾ liter
Length	in.	inches	2.54	centimeters	⅜ in.	= 1 cm	
	ft	feet	30.48	centimeters	1 in.	= 2.5 cm	
	yd	yards	0.9144	meters	2 in.	= 5 cm	
	mi	miles	1.609	kilometers	2½ in.	= 6.5 cm	
	km	kilometers	0.621	miles	12 in. (1 ft)	= 30 cm	
	m	meters	1.094	yards	1 yd	= 90 cm	
	cm	centimeters	0.39	inches	100 ft	= 30 m	
					1 mi	= 1.6 km	
Temperature	° F	Fahrenheit	5/9 (after subtracting 32)	Celsius	32° F	= 0° C	
					68°F	= 20°C	
	° C	Celsius	9/5 (then add 32)	Fahrenheit	212° F	= 100° C	
Area	in.^{2}	square inches	6.452	square centimeters	1 in.^{2}	= 6.5 cm^2	
	ft^2	square feet	929.0	square centimeters	1 ft^2	= 930 cm^2	
	yd^2	square yards	8361.0	square centimeters	1 yd^2	= 8360 cm^2	
	a.	acres	0.4047	hectares	1 a.	= 4050 m^2	

INDEX

Page numbers in boldface type indicate principal references; page numbers in italic type indicate references to illustrations.